This book is drawn from discussions that have taken place in the American Theatre Wing *Working in the Theatre* programs, a fixture in the New York City theatre community for more than three decades. A unique opportunity for theatre artists to engage in sustained conversations about the field, the seminars were begun in the early 1970s by ATW president Isabelle Stevenson, as panel discussions taking place at theatres around the city, pioneering the idea of allowing audiences to hear directly from artists and administrators about the creation of theatre. Since 1979, ATW has partnered with CUNY TV, the television arm of The City University of New York, to bring these discussions into homes throughout New York City, and beginning in 2003, the programs have been available to audiences internationally on the Internet via both the ATW and CUNY TV Web sites.

The seminars on which this book is based were hosted or moderated by Ben Cameron, Theodore S. Chapin, Thomas Cott, Dasha Epstein, Brendan Gill, Sondra Gilman, Martin Gottfried, Mel Gussow, Jeffrey Eric Jenkins, Doug Leeds, Pia Lindström, Lonny Price, Harvey Sabinson, Howard Sherman, Roy A. Somlyo, Isabelle Stevenson, Peter Stone, and George C. White.

Also from Continuum in the *Working in the Theatre* series is *Acting*, and others devoted to Writing and Directing are planned.

# Producing and the Theatre Business

# Producing & the Theatre Business

## WORKING IN THE THEATRE


EDITED BY
Robert Emmet Long

FOREWORD BY
Elizabeth Ireland McCann


AMERICAN
THEATRE
WING
Founder of the Tony Awards®




A GINIGER BOOK

continuum

NEW YORK • LONDON

2007

The Continuum International Publishing Group Inc
80 Maiden Lane, New York, NY 10038

The Continuum International Publishing Group Ltd
The Tower Building, 11 York Road, London SE1 7NX

The K. S. Giniger Company Inc
250 West 57 Street, New York NY 10107

www.continuum-books.com



Printed in the United States of America

Library of Congress Cataloging-in-Publication Data

Producing and the theatre business : working in the theatre / edited by Robert Emmet Long ; foreword by Elizabeth McCann.
p. cm.
A Giniger book
Includes index.
ISBN-13: 978-0-8264-1810-4 (hardcover : alk. paper)
ISBN-10: 0-8264-1810-4 (hardcover : alk. paper)
ISBN-13: 978-0-8264-1811-1 (pbk. : alk. paper)
ISBN-10: 0-8264-1811-2 (pbk. : alk. paper)
1. Theater—Production and direction. I. Long, Robert Emmet. II. Title.

PN2053.P73 2007
792.02'32—dc22

2007001801

green press INITIATIVE

Continuum is committed to preserving ancient forests and natural resources. In keeping with this effort, this book has been printed on 30% postconsumer waste recycled paper.

# *Contents*

# *Foreword by Elizabeth Ireland McCann*

As the managing producer of Tony Award Productions, and as an eight-time Tony recipient, I spend a lot of time asking others about what those awards mean—to those in our profession, to those who fill our theatres, even to those who stumble across it on CBS one Sunday night each June. In my highly idiosyncratic, undeniably personal survey, I have come to find that for every person I ask, there is a different answer; so I keep on asking, because I enjoy hearing what others think, and wrestling with the unknown.

That said, although the people whose voices and thoughts make up this volume may not be familiar to you, they are all well-known to me. After all, professional theatre in America is a relatively small community, and the Broadway region is even smaller, made up of a very select few city blocks. Those of us who create theatre on Broadway encounter each other almost daily in theatres, coffee shops, meetings, and dashing through Shubert Alley, in the Times Square area that is, at least come eight o'clock most nights, the home to almost every potential Tony Award recipient.

We know of each other's successes and failures; we know each other's theatrical tastes; we have all done business with each other on some level or another, and in all likelihood, we will do so again one day. But the fact is, when we see each other, our conversation focuses on the business at hand, or the news of the day. After all, there is work to be done, and always too little time in which to do it.

That is what makes the American Theatre Wing's program so unique. Every so often, we're invited to come together, in the middle of the day, to talk with each other not about what we're doing today or tomorrow. Instead, we talk about *how* we go about our business and, perhaps even more intriguingly, *why*.

The *Working in the Theatre* panels are, so I'm told, designed to help students and the public learn more about the making of theatre. I think they do help to demystify our business in a way that makes it less glamorous or exotic, but has the benefit of making it accessible. They help our audiences look beyond merely the success or failure of a specific show to—and here are those words again—how and why that show came to be.

What's remarkable to me, whether I'm on a panel or catch some of my peers on one while watchng at home, is that for so many of us, this is the first opportunity we've all had to interact with each other on this kind of reflective, philosophical level, to share our knowledge, our experience, and, most of all, our common passion for the theatre not only with the audience, but with each other.

As I read through this book, I am delighted to find new answers, and to make the acquaintance of so many friends whom I mistakenly thought I knew.

# *Introduction*

This volume is drawn from the American Theatre Wing archive of transcripts from the popular discussion series of *Working in the Theatre* seminars. Since the sessions are not formal, the term *seminars* may be somewhat misleading. Rather, they are extemporaneous, freewheeling, and great fun. At the same time, these programs are always highly informative.

Theatre is a creative and collaborative enterprise. But like any enterprise in a capitalistic culture, it must rely on the initial flow of money from entrepreneurs and investors. There can be an uneasy relationship between commerce and creativity. But the relationship is a dynamic one. An aim of *Producing and the Theatre Business* is to demystify the work of producers and many others connected with the financial end of theatre.

In the popular imagination, producers are usually thought of as an elite class of money handlers, the makers of "product"; distant, less-than-creative businesspeople or even mere bean-counters, having little affinity for art. Such a conception would be simplistic and utterly misguided. Producers are more often as passionately committed to the theatre as anyone on the creative team. They are risk-takers, gambling against great odds that their investments will show a profit. They could find safer ways to invest their money. But the stage excites their blood. Making a strike in the glamorous world of the New York or London stage is the biggest strike of all. Producers must have an eye for talent among writers, directors, actors, publicists, and managers. As Oscar Hammerstein observed: "A producer is a rare, paradoxical genius: hard-headed, soft-hearted, cautious, reckless, a hopeful innocent in fair weather, a stern pilot in stormy weather, an idealist, a realist, a practical dreamer, a sophisticated gambler, a stage-struck child."

The role of the producer involves the reader in a large and complex world. The prototypical producer of the 1950s—exemplified by the one-man-rules-all showmanship of a David Merrick or George Abbott—has for the most part disappeared. In his place (then it was always a "he"), among other figures, are the corporate investors, who have the deep pockets needed to stage long-running, blockbuster musicals.

The process of funding a new production may well be difficult and slow. A show may not reach Broadway or the West End for years. Before it does, it may be taken on the road—a gambit that is likely to cost well over a million dollars today, but that provides an opportunity to learn from audiences where the weaknesses are. They then rewrite, perhaps almost to the opening night, before the show is premiered in New York. Even revivals can be complicated to stage, being presented in times that are very different from their first production.

In this book, one hears the voices of many people with whom the producer must work. He or she must interact, for instance, with management firms and a general manager in particular, who is selected to put the production together under his or her supervision. The producer must accommodate unions, which have strict rules. Also explored from several points of view is the role of the critic—with particular attention to how the opinions of members of the print and other media, including the influence of the Internet, relate to marketing, the creation of "buzz," and the ultimate financial success or failure of a show as measured by the length of its run.

*Producing and the Theatre Business* includes "in depth" edited excerpts from programs on the financial and artistic challenges faced and overcome in bringing recent hit shows to the Broadway stage. These entertaining and illuminating give-and-take excerpts help to give the reader a sense of what it is the producer does. Excerpted seminars include *Avenue Q, The Drowsy Chaperone, Hairspray, Mamma Mia!, The Producers,* and *Thoroughly Modern Millie.*

A few words about the process of turning fleeting conversation into the permanence of a book are appropriate. The excerpts have been organized to bring together and place into high relief recurring themes from more than three decades of broadcast transcripts, and in so doing to create a compact volume consisting of as many voices as possible to showcase the business process of theatrical art. Often, comparable or contrasting views and anecdotes are arranged for maximum effect. Synthesizing many thousands of pages of conversation, literally from different eras, into one modest-sized volume has been a challenge. Some of the individual excerpts, as well as the in-depth sections, have been lightly edited to provide maximum fluency in the conversations. Basic biographical sketches and an index are included for easy reference.

Economics has been called *the dismal science.* Yet, this book is as much about the excitement found in dreaming about and creating theatre as it is about money matters. A producer, speaking for many theatre people, says that her greatest thrill, and the reason that she is a producer, is to see something that exists at first as an idea come into full bloom as a beautiful and unforgettable stage creation.

Robert Emmet Long

# Producing and the Theatre Business

1

# What Is a Producer?

*Elizabeth McCann*

We're in the business of making something out of nothing. That's what we do. We take a piece of paper and we read it. And a director says, "I can spin a web with that piece of paper." We make a total commitment of faith.

We are the last of the believers I always think.

I have a great fondness for producers. I don't like them because they're my competition. But I admire the tenacity that makes them do that. I don't think there's one producer that couldn't have a more relaxed life and probably, financially, a more rewarding life someplace else.

*Richard Frankel*

It's all on-the-job training. For all of us.

*Robert Barandes*

The person who orchestrates it all is the producer. He's going to have to raise the money—and to raise money, you have to have a dream you can sell, which you can give to people in a fashion that they can understand why this deserves an investment. And that's a hard thing to do.

*Elizabeth Williams*

What we are doing is an interesting blend of commerce and art. And obviously, the two have to be perfectly balanced.

*Amy Nederlander*

When a producer is considering a project, one has to respond to it oneself and be passionate about it. You need to have that passion, to make other people care. If you choose something because, *Oh, it has someone famous in it,* but you don't really like it, the public's going to know that. The press is going to know that. It's not going to work. You're the driving force. You're choosing your director, collaborating and choosing the creative team. And you have to love what you're doing.

*David Stone*

Producing is about balance. That's the art of it: being able to follow the passion of the artists, giving them what they need and getting completely taken away by the process of it, the creative process, but still being able to make proper business decisions. And it's easy to just do the art, as a producer. We've seen, perhaps, producers who have just maybe done things that weren't right, in terms of business decisions. And it's easy just to look at the bottom line. The hardest thing is to navigate between the two.

### *Fran Weissler*

A show starts out with somebody finding out what the project is. Now, that's the first thing that a producer has to do, to find out *What are we producing?* There are a million ways that that happens, and that something comes to you. We are the muscle, certainly first, because we pick the director, the scenic designers, and the costumers with the director, and so on, to make it happen.

But then, the first day you walk into that rehearsal room, it's the director. The producer has to relinquish a lot of what she does and give it over to the director. Ultimately, it all becomes the property of the audience. We have to give it up, but we do begin it all.

### *Daryl Roth*

What you need is the passion to produce. You need to be able to raise money. If it's not your own money, you need to supplement it with investors, so you have to share that enthusiasm.

### *Elizabeth McCann*

First of all, a playwright needs a producer. A playwright has a vision. He has something he wants to tell a group of people, collectively. Now, he's not a novelist. He doesn't sit home alone, write a novel, and send it off to a publisher and maybe get it published.

A play cannot be realized without producers. Producers who come along and contract the actors, pay the bills, develop an advertising campaign, and do all of the things that are necessary for that writer's voice to be heard.

That's what we do.

Now, we do it all on Broadway in a very sophisticated way. But that is not the only way to produce. I've known young actors who found a play that they wanted to see, and they hassled their families into putting up ten-thousand dollars, which may seem like a lot; and they found a loft and they did it. They were producers. They just did it. We have graduated up the line to doing it on a more sophisticated or higher-risk-venture.

### *Alan Schuster*

The essential difference between the theatre and every other medium is the theatre is a writer's medium. The ownership of the material rests with the authors. We can try and change the material as producers, but we don't own it. It's not like the movie business, in which the material is owned by the producers.

Musicals are much more collaborative than straight plays. But even in this case, it is the vision of the author, lyricist, and composer that comes through. Not our vision.

### *Thomas Viertel*

Of course, the trick in being a producer to some extent is to have that passion and understand it, because obviously we wind up sharing that passion with the audience of anything that we go through to produce, while still remaining businesslike.

*Richard Frankel*

There always is a designated hitter, so to speak, that all of the producers give their notes to. And we pride ourselves, on all of our shows, that we don't bother the artists, that we protect the artists against the opinions of everyone else. The producers speak with one voice. Any arguments that they have between them are fought, but privately. And then, someone is designated to go talk to the artists about it.

*Emanuel Azenberg*

I don't really want to walk backstage into an antagonistic situation. Also, I think I am old enough to be idealistic now, and I think that the truth is a lot easier. So there's no illusion, no *the producer is someone that people have to be afraid of*. We walk backstage, we keep everybody in the company abreast of all the economics, so that there is no rumor. This industry is rife with rumors, and you hear stories on a daily basis. It's better to—old military expression—keep the troops informed. So, we keep the troops informed, and also, we are accessible, so that if anyone has a complaint that person comes up and articulates it. It doesn't mean that I'm going to agree. It just means that they're not afraid to ask.

*Bernard Gersten*

We bill ourselves: "Lincoln Center Theater is under the direction of André Bishop and Bernard Gersten." André is responsible for the core artistic decisions. He is the person responsible for the repertory and artists. It's like an A&R [Artists & Repertoire] person. Nobody says, "A&R," but it is A&R.

The responsibilities of the administration, marketing, fundraising, and financing of the theatre are primarily my responsibility.

*Julianne Boyd*

The producing organization used to be an entirely different entity. There were producers who did nothing but theatre, and they had the general managers and the press agents, and so forth. They developed the scripts. Now, oftentimes, the scripts go to the director. The director then works with the playwright developing the script.

It then goes to a producer, because the producers may be on Wall Street. And you try to find someone who has money.

*Robert Barandes*

When I first started as an attorney in the theatre business a producer was sitting with me, who will remain nameless, and he said, "Finding creative people in the theatre is very difficult." And I, being very young at the time, said, "Yes, the artist, the director, the writers—impossible." He said, "Nah, they're technical. Creative is raising the money."

*Bernard Gersten*

Producers have very, very slight reputations in reality, except for a handful of flamboyant producers. So that people may have known when they went to a David Merrick show, years ago, because David cut a swath. I don't know how many people knew, or know, that they're going to see a Cameron Mackintosh production.

*Elizabeth McCann*

David Merrick used the expression, "Who has the muscle?" David always said he had the muscle. But on a Jerome Robbins show, Jerome Robbins had the muscle. It meant somebody had to be in charge and have a clear idea of the vision.

*Mel Brooks*

I produced a lot of movies, and I know what it takes to be a producer. It takes a love of what you're doing. Without the love, it's just business.

*Susan Gallin*

To me, the experience of a play and why I produce a play is because the people go into the theatre and they have an experience. They are sparked to think about something. They're elevated in a way that doesn't happen if you see that play on film. And if you see the same idea translated into a television show, it's a plot. It's a story. It's not about something that's going to enlighten you in some way. Maybe that's an idealistic way of thinking what theatre is.

*Tisa Chang*

You have to be willing to take responsibility, I think that's what it is. You have to love to take responsibility as a producer, because I now understand how difficult it is.

As a performer, I never could quite understand what went on behind the scenes. But in producing, one really has to have the acumen of business as well as an aesthetic sense; and deal with people. Just the unions and the paperwork, the fundraising, the marketing—it's just amazing. So, it is juggling a lot of balls.

*Charlotte Wilcox*

Really, the only way to train is through experience. When I started, you couldn't go to college to learn any management courses. I don't think there were any at that time. Now, you have them everywhere. They're certainly valuable and helpful.

And then, you still have to go to a manager's office and work: the budgeting process first with an idea of what the negotiating will involve, since that's the only way you can budget. Then, the reality of what each item costs varies slightly once you actually start those negotiations. You don't get into numbers of people and so forth except in terms of your cast, specifically, since you don't know what your physical production is going to be until you get there. And that determines the number of people you use.

*David Stone*

Any time I've produced anything, thinking, *You know what? This is going to work. This is going to make money. I'm going to do this because . . .* , it's never worked. And anytime I've said, *I just love this, I don't care if it works, I love it,* it always has.

*Susan Gallin*

People say it's hard to find investors. They're there. When you have something, if you believe in it, they're there, and they're the passionate people. We're passionate about what we do. Those investors are passionate about theatre too, and want to support us.

*Joseph Stein*

There are very few theatres available and very few producers. As a matter of fact, in order to do a show, the producers outnumber the cast. When Frank Loesser was being produced, they had one producer. *Fiddler on the Roof* was produced by one producer. Now, it's a matter of getting eight or ten people together, or fifteen—I don't even know who they are—in order to get a show staged.

*Harold Prince*

Creative producers have been driven out of the theatre. [Why do I think so?] Because I was a creative producer. Because I wouldn't know how to raise money standing on my head stark naked in Times Square. All I had to do was raise a little bit of money from a lot of loving people who adored the theatre. There are fewer of those, and I could not come up with ten-million dollars today, with my reputation—not remotely. And I wouldn't know how to go about it because I wouldn't want to make the moves you have to make to get that kind of money. The costs have driven the right people out. Now, there are exceptions. But we're not here to talk about exceptions.

*Lloyd Richards*

I don't know what happened to those marvelous old producers who used to take a writer under his or her wing and support him or her in development, and assist in his or her development—but they disappeared.

*Emanuel Azenberg*

My first recommendation is that you find something that you care about and you feel that expresses something of yourself. I know that's not chic for producers, but I think it's certainly crucial and certainly part of the way I was trained. Subsequent to that, you have to option the piece, or you have to own it in a sense. Your obligation is to be very helpful artistically, to the extent that you can be, and to the extent that your peripheral position—which is what a producer is, in the creation of a piece—allows you to be.

You're fully responsible for the economics. And you have to go out and raise a lot of money, which is sometimes difficult, but sometimes more embarrassing—because it's not really an investment. It's a crapshoot. And it's a cultural crapshoot, which in my mind justifies it for myself—we're trying to do something that might nudge the world. That's a Stoppard line, it's not mine.

That heartfelt commitment justifies your behavior.

*Marvin Hamlisch*

For me, Broadway is supposed to be about taking a chance. It's not supposed to be about always bringing in something that you know was a hit somewhere, so therefore, *We can't lose.* To me, it is the roll of the dice. I don't think they knew that *West Side Story* was going to be *WEST SIDE STORY.*

*Bernard Gersten*

Most everybody in the world who's likely to be listening knows what productions are. People decide—on the basis of reading or listening, or some combination of reading and hearing, or listening to somebody tell a story, or being handed a script, or listening to a bunch of songs—that they're going to produce a play or a musical. You assemble money or you're an institutional theatre and you do it in a slightly different way.

*Amy Nederlander*

When people ask, "Well, what do you do? What does a producer do?," the shorthand of that is: nothing happens without the producer making it happen. Either they're doing it themselves, sweeping the floor, or they're delegating it. But they know everything that's going on, and it's happening because they've made it happen.

*Ian McKellen*

In England, the director is supreme. In America, the producer is.

## IN DEPTH: *The Producers* (2001)

*(Included in this discussion are producer Mel Brooks; producer Richard Frankel; Laura Green, general manager; co-author Thomas Meehan; and director and choreographer Susan Stroman.)*

### Mel Brooks

The Producers *was a movie. We all know there was a movie called, originally,* Springtime for Hitler *and then called* The Producers *because Joseph E. Levine, whose company distributed the film and put up half the money for it, called all of the exhibitors in America, who were Jewish at that time, and asked, "What about 'Springtime for Hitler'?" The reaction was, "Not on my marquee!" He asked me for another title and I didn't fight him. I said, "Joe, you're right. I mean, unless you know the work, just to throw that title up there would be off-putting to say the least."*

*So, I thought of a kind of salute and irony at the same time in calling these two guys "The Producers." And it's been* The Producers *since then. That was 1967.*

*I guess you want the true story. Years and years ago, I worked for a fellow. He used to do shows. Every one of them was a flop. He never had a hit. And he raised money by making love to these dowagers, these widows who would give him money. And they'd write out the checks to the name of the play, which was always "Cash."*

*And I worked for him. He wore a kind of charcoal-gray alpaca coat—in the winter, in the summer. And he wore a producer's hat. He was never without his little producer's homburg. He was an unforgettable character, and I loved him.*

ATW

*I think it is generally known that you brought the script of the Broadway musical to David Geffen.*

Mel Brooks

*I didn't bring the script. He started it all. There was no script. He really was responsible. But he had to bow out. He was running DreamWorks. He has much to be proud of. They do wonderful work. He's a hands-on guy. He said, even though he started it, he called and said, "You have got to do* The Producers, *it's a natural for a Broadway musical." And he got as involved as he could, and then he said, "I can't really be a hands-on producer." And so, he said, "Just get me a couple of tickets for opening night."*

ATW

*Richard, you're a producer of the show and there are others as well. How did you get involved in bringing the show to Broadway?*

Richard Frankel

*After the long process of Mel and Stro and Mike Ockrent putting the show together and writing it, they had a reading. And after the reading, faced with all the enthusiasm of every producer in town, basically interviewed—more or less auditioned—all the producers to pick the people they wanted. And we were chosen.*

* * *

## MEL BROOKS

*When David Geffen actually gave us the bad news that he wouldn't produce the show, about a week before our reading, we got Nathan Lane to do it. We got Gary Beach to do it. We got Cady Huffman to do it. And we got a couple of other people. Glen Kelly, our musical supervisor and arranger, was at the piano. And we did this incredible reading—first reading to the world of* The Producers. *Laura, Richard, and Rocco Landesman were invited. We had to assemble a bunch of producers in a hurry.*

## SUSAN STROMAN

*We had a studio and we had these actors, and we did it ourselves, really. Made some personal phone calls to producers that we'd worked with and admired, and we had them come in and listen to our reading. We needed to find a producer of* The Producers. *That was in April 2000. So this happened quite fast.*

## THOMAS MEEHAN

*Everyone loved it and the money was raised. But the other thing was, we saw a lot of flaws. And we worked very hard to fix them. We did a lot of work with new songs.*

MEL BROOKS

*It was not a hit, I can tell you. Not then.*

ATW

*Richard, what was the next step? You decided who the producers would be?*

RICHARD FRANKEL

*No. We all got together and tried to figure out a sensible financial strategy for it.*

MEL BROOKS

*Let me tell you about the producers. We sat and decided instead of having one maniac producer [we would have a team]. I didn't beg. I demanded. I said, "You can't come onboard if we can't go out of town." Because when you go out of town, not only do you work out the kinks and the bad stuff, and cut it out and put new stuff in, but the actors get to bond. They love each other. They work so much better, you can see the love onstage. They're familiar with the material, they love their costumes, their parts. And when they come into New York, they come in as a unit instead of a disparate bunch of actors with egos, fighting with each other.*

*Out of town is critical. If you're ever going to do a show, take it out of town, or don't do the show. Don't to it.*

*We talked about the symbiotic relationship of the producers to the work itself. Richard loved* The Producers. *Rocco Landesman, who runs the Jujamcyn Theatres, grabbed me and said,*

*"I love this show. You have the St. James Theatre if you want it." I said, "OK, you're in. You're one of the producers."*

*Then, we said,* We have got to go on the road one of these days, we need a distribution producer, somebody who knows how to take a show on the road. *There's a company called SFX—they do that, and they do it brilliantly.*

*Then there was this guy, Robert Sillerman, who ran SFX, and then sold it and ran it and sold it, a very wise, bright guy who loved the show so much that I said, "Just for your love alone, and your two-billion dollars"—he's one of the richest guys on earth—I said, "You're in."*

### ATW

*At some point, you had to decide how much money to raise. You must have had a target and then had an idea how to reach it.*

### Richard Frankel

*It cost us almost $2,000,000 to go to Chicago, $2,000,000 extra. Whereas we had been thinking in the beginning that the show might cost eight or eight-and-a-half, after contemplating going out of town, we decided that we had better raise ten-and-a-half. Mel was completely right—it seemed like the completely sensible thing to do. In fact, it would seem utterly foolish and suicidal not to go out of town and test the jokes, and have the cast bond. It was $2,000,000 well worth spending.*

### ATW

*You then created a budget?*

RICHARD FRANKEL

*Pages. I don't know: twenty, thirty pages of budget.*

ATW

*Had you formed a production company at this point, a limited partnership?*

RICHARD FRANKEL

*Yes, we had formed a joint venture among the producers and were beginning to form a limited partnership. . . .*

*It takes a village. Bialystock didn't do shows that cost ten-and-a-half-million dollars. Times weren't as complicated as these are today. We have, over the years, produced forty to forty-five shows. We have four- to five-hundred people who invest with us. We encourage them to invest relatively modest amounts of money. And we go to them when we're about to do a project, and we tell them about the project and tell them if they're interested to contact us. In this instance, we had $2,000,000 to raise and $4,000,000 of interest arrived within four days.*

MEL BROOKS

*We had more backers than we could get in.*

ATW

*What caused this buzz?*

Richard Frankel

*Oh, the movie is beloved. Mel is beloved. Stro, Tom, the entire project had a lot of heat. And you only had to mention* The Producers. *Mel Brooks wrote the music, Stro, everything else—and people responded instantly.*

*About half of the people who wanted to invest did. We had our two-hundred people. There are a few attractive old ladies. There are dentists and stockbrokers, and all sorts of nice people.*

ATW

*Each put up about $10,000?*

Richard Frankel

*Each—we restricted it to $10,000. People wanted to invest more. But we wanted to involve as many people as we could.*

ATW

*In the forty-five shows that you've done, have you ever encountered anything like that before?*

Richard Frankel

*Never. Never. We had had a few modest successes. But truth be told, you are not prepared for this. What we prepare for, what producers and general managers prepare for, is survival in the face of catastrophe. That's what we're good at. That's what requires all the skill—making the show work when the circum-*

*stances are less-than-perfect. That's what we train for and that's what we practice. This leaves one somewhat unprepared, this kind of success.*

* * *

## Mel Brooks

*When I first came in to do* The Producers, *my first vision of it was basically what David Geffen had seen originally. It was* The Producers, *the movie, on the stage with music. You needed "Springtime for Hitler" and maybe you needed "Prisoners of Love." But certainly, you needed one or two songs, and it would have been a play with music. Then when I met Tom Meehan—Tom who had done* Annie *and some other wonderful stuff on Broadway, Tom said, "No, no, no. A musical is a musical."*

*Then, we met Mike Ockrent and he said, "Well, you need a curtain-raiser." I asked, "What's that?" "Well, it's a little number at the top of the show that says* Hello *to the audience. And you have to end the first act with a great big production number."*

*Then I said, "Oh, I get it."*

*Stro showed me what the audience wants and needs on Broadway, a musical comedy. It has to sing. It has to dance. It has to have beautiful girls. It has to look splendid. It has to be rich. It has to really thrill the audience for two hours, two-and-a-half hours.*

## ATW

*As a producer, you've seen shows in all kinds of trouble and with all kinds of friction. Why not so in this one?*

### Richard Frankel

*We saw early on, and within the confines of the financial structure, basically our role: service providers. Our job is to give [the creative team] what they need. That's what we are here to do. What they need, also, is to stay within a financial context so that the show can work financially—for the participants and the investors. But basically, we all saw our job as giving them what will help them to do their best work.*

* * *

### ATW

*I'm sure when you made a budget of ten-and-a-half-million dollars, you knew what you were talking about at the time.*

### Laura Green

*And there's a reserve built in there.*

### Richard Frankel

*Yes. It's not to say that there wasn't a dialogue between the designer and ourselves, and Stro and Mel, about what we could afford and what we can't afford—and how do we get this? If we really need this, we have to give up that. But the process seemed to work. . . .*

*The biggest reason is that we didn't throw out any songs. It turned out that all the characters were fully formed. It wasn't as if characters had to be rewritten. Songs would then have had to be rewritten, things moved from one act to another. We had no major structural changes to the script—and if we had had major structural changes to the script, it no doubt would have resulted in big scenery changes and big costume changes.*

## ATW

*Don't you think it's important for all shows to go out of town and to have this in the budget?*

## Richard Frankel

*The sad fact is that on many projects you just can't afford it. What you have is a much less-perfect solution, which is preview a long time in New York. It would have been terrible in our instance, and we could afford, because of the quality of the participants and the quality of the material, to go out of town. It's absolutely what every show and producer should do in the best of all possible worlds.*

2

# In the Beginning

*Daryl Roth*

You have to have a product. You have to have a play. You have to have whatever it is.

*Terrence McNally*

It's like trying to grow an orchid in Alaska, for a play to blossom. There are so many things that can go wrong.

*Elizabeth Williams*

You have to structure it from the beginning so that you, in some way, have that control.

*Kevin McCollum*

One of the things I tell people when they say, "Oh, hey, I've got the money for the show, let's do it" is, "Well, tell me about the money." The reason I ask about it is I won't take anybody as an investor until I've really spent some time with him or her and had lunch, and they get to know me—because God forbid you have a hit.

There's expensive money and inexpensive money. And if you're going to be a producer in the commercial theatre, and if there's somebody who's willing to write you a check, you have to go to lunch with him or her. You have to spend time with them, talk about their belief system, get to know them a little bit, because—again—god forbid it's a hit. Failures take care of themselves. Everyone loves each other on a failure. *Oh, it was great. Oh, I love you.*

Five years down the line, if you're a hit and you're not getting along, it's a problem.

### *Daryl Roth*

Projects come in so many different ways. That's one way that commercial producers might move forward. There's another way. You could start with an idea on the other end of the spectrum and take it to a director and a writer. There's square one. There's another way: you can just read a play that was sent to you. There's another way, you have relationships with playwrights, and you do one play of theirs and they come to you with the next play. You want to build relationships and loyalty, so you go that way. There are so many ways that plays are born.

### *Nancy Nagel Gibbs*

We need to cultivate what can't be cloned on TV. That's what sets us apart.

But I don't know how to clone it. I don't know how to tell an author and others in the creative end how to make that happen. It's something that's organically in the material, and hopefully we as producers spot it and can make it economically viable in order to make it happen.

## *Harold Prince*

You do something and you think, *I don't know whether this is going to work.* Then you see it, and it doesn't or it does. And then you move on from there. It's as if you were making the rules as you go along.

That is not always the case. This is parenthetical and maybe even seemingly irrelevant, but when I go to work in London, because they're not used to this process, the only rule I ever have is that the show that previews the first night is going to be the show, because we'll never be able to fix it afterward. That's my experience—that's the show, because in London they just don't have that experience.

## *Kevin McCollum*

If you create something from scratch and with original characters, a corporation is very interested in investing not just for what happens on Broadway, but because when you are that initial producer in the live theatre, there is an incredible bundle of rights that get activated. Many corporations are interested in investing, and they'll say, "Fine for Broadway. But you know what? We'd love to have a first look at electronic media."

A lot of these corporations will find a complementary relationship in what you're doing and what their core business is. We're seeing that more and more.

A lot of producers take that money as a hedge against the future, but a lot of producers also find it offensive because they're saying, "Look, I'm taking the risk. Let's see what happens, and then I'll come to you if there's something we can do together." It just varies on the personality of the producer and the kind of project.

Corporations that are producers have other agendas then just necessarily the Broadway production.

## *Richard Frankel*

The main difference between rights to a play and rights to a film, from the writer, is that in a play you obtain very particular rights from the author, and everything that you don't obtain specifically from the author, he or she keeps: whereas in a film, usually, it's a work for hire. The writer is paid and then the person doing the film owns everything connected with it.

So, in the case of a play, you basically obtain the right to present the play live before an audience. And if you successfully do that in New York, you then can obtain the rights to present the play in London or Canada or Europe, or somewhere else. But the basic idea is that you're only taking those rights. Other things, like movie rights, book rights, and all of that stay with the authors in a play.

## *Robert Barandes*

You sometimes have different groups that have to get paid. We actually refer to our authors on [*Damn Yankees*] by two different names. The authors are the people who wrote it, and the owners are the people who get paid. Some of the authors are no longer with us, some are. And the owners may be their estates, may be beneficiaries that now get paid. In terms of negotiating the numbers, however, the numbers are pretty much the same, though they're distributed differently.

*Berenice Weiler*

A producer, when he or she finds his or her piece of material will hire a general-management firm. It used to be, years ago, that the producers who worked year-round would have a GM on their staff on a year-round basis. But now, they don't do it as often. And I have said many times that general managers now audition for their jobs since the producers go around to various managers looking for them, and decide whom they would like to hire.

*Fran Weissler*

It is about falling in love. We fell in love with a play called *Falsettos,* which nobody wanted to produce, nobody wanted to direct—nobody would give us a theatre. It was Jewish, it was homosexual, it was about AIDS. So, those are three things that nobody was interested in. And nobody realized what a genius Bill Finn was, and how incredible his music was, and how funny it was. At the ending, of course, you got a kick in the stomach. But it was just an amazing show. And just to get it started, I used to sing the lyrics. I used to be in the shower with it. I used to cry every time I read it, and nobody would give us the time of day.

Ultimately, we put all our own money in it, except for one theatre owner, who made us sign personally—so that if we failed, we would lose everything. We gambled our entire careers on that show. I don't think I ever said that before, but we could have been out of business.

And when, indeed, the Tonys came and we won the Best Composer, the Best Lyricist, and the Best Book—we didn't win Best Musical—it was a very exciting moment for us to have gotten those awards. And because it was all our money, we got it back in twenty-six weeks, which is unheard of.

## *Kevin McCollum*

I get teased a lot for a quote I use, "We're in the drug business," which it is, and the drug we're trying to create is the kind that gets the hair on the back of your neck to stand up. I always say, if it's a five-hair-on-the-neck-standing-up in a musical, you might have a shot. It might not be logical in terms of business, since it doesn't fit any formula—and I'm anti-formula, anyway. But it's what you're thirsty for and you don't know you're thirsty for. It's that kind of, *Oh, that surprised me.* And if you're going to spend a hundred dollars on a ticket, there better be five really wonderful, emotional surprises to your story.

## *Thomas Viertel*

I keep coming back to the idea that this is a business about emotions. You cannot get a hundred dollars from people for treating them to a piece of intellectual material. You have to get it because you were touching them in ways that television can't and, generally speaking, movies can't. Without that, I don't think you've got anything on which to base a show.

*Gregory Hines*

*Jelly's Last Jam* was a breakthrough. There were elements that were shocking, disturbing, yet very original. Potential investors were therefore hesitant to invest since, they thought, it was too dark—no pun intended.

*Elizabeth McCann*

I can remember the time when the Shuberts took a risk on *Cats*. Now, you look at me and ask, "*Cats* was a risk?" Yes, it was at the moment. People said, "You don't want to produce a musical with T. S. Eliot lyrics. Come on." I can remember the late Bernie Jacobs [of The Shubert Organization] taking the London cast album of *Cats* and playing it for his grandchildren, and coming back saying, "Kids can understand this." There is no foolproof formula. Every time I've done something that can't miss, it blows up in my face—without fail.

*Cy Feuer*

Every show Ernie Martin and I have done—with the exception of *The Boy Friend*, which we found in London—the idea was one that we came up with. It was our idea. Then, we would cast the writers. And it was a battle.

## *Charles Strouse*

I've always had trouble. But everybody does. Leonard Bernstein had trouble. I used to play auditions at *West Side Story*, so I know how much trouble there was to get that on.

*Bye Bye Birdie* was [shopped around] about five-and-a-half years, and nobody would take any interest in that. We played it for anybody. We'd pick people off the street corner: "Come see our new show."

It's only different today in the fact that there are no people like Cy Feuer around, who will say, "I don't care what. I think you guys are great, and I'm passionate about this idea. I'll get the six-or-eight-million dollars. I'll do it." There's nobody around like that.

## *André Bishop*

I called Susan Stroman. I had cleared the way with her beloved agent, Flora Roberts, and I called her up. And I asked, "Would you be interested in coming in and talking to me about a show?" I guess she could have said, "No." But she said, "Yes," and she came in and we talked. And then she went away and I didn't hear from her for months and months and months.

Suddenly, one day she called and she said, "Well, I've been thinking about your offer. And I do have an idea, and I've talked with John Weidman"—whom I had known since we produced *Assassins*, when I was working at Playwrights Horizons—"and we would like to come in and talk to you about an idea we have."

So, they came in. And we talked about this idea that turned out to be the basis of the third piece in the play, in the evening, called *Contact*. And it was loosely based on a short story by Ambrose Bierce.

And you know, when guys like me have meetings with people like them and they recount the plot of what they want to do, it always sounds awful. The plot of *Hamlet* sounds boring. But what you do is you say, "Oh, that sounds wonderful!," because you believe in the talented people.

### *Elizabeth McCann*

Nobody can be conned quicker than a producer. I can be conned by a director. I can be conned by a writer quicker than anybody, with all the experience I've had. So, it's about falling in love. You just fall in love. And the most, I think, thrilling moment for Daryl Roth and me was the first time we heard an Edward Albee play read aloud, and no one had heard it before but us.

## IN DEPTH: *The Drowsy Chaperone* (2006)

*(Included in this discussion are lyricist Lisa Lambert, producer Kevin McCollum, director Bob Martin, and producer Roy Miller.)*

### ATW

*It isn't often that a wedding present becomes a Broadway musical, and even more rare that a completely Canadian musical reaches Broadway. How did it all begin?*

## Bob Martin

*It has been an extraordinary journey. I was getting married to Janet Van De Graaff, who's an actress. Janet and I saw an ad in a local paper for a show at a club in downtown Toronto called the Rivoli, and the show was called* Oh, What a Pair, *which was kind of an inside joke about a fake show title that we had suggested for an awkwardly titled show—it's a joke among friends.*

*But the evening was called,* Oh, What a Pair, *and it consisted of two acts, the first being sort of stand-up routines and sort of little comic moments during which friends from the theatre-and-comedy communities did a little tribute to my wife and myself. The second half was called* The Drowsy Chaperone, *which was about forty minutes long. It was basically a 1920s musical, fully costumed.*

## ATW

*It was Lisa Lambert and Greg Morrison, composers of the music and lyrics, and Don McKellar, writer of the book, who had cooked this whole thing up?*

## Lisa Lambert

*Yes, it was the three of us, plus there was a group of comedy and theatre people who were friends of ours in Toronto, who were part of this whole thing, too. We all cooked it up together—and thought of it as a one-night event.*

### Bob Martin

*It was originally thought of as a one-off thing.*

### ATW

*Roy, you heard about a show in Toronto. And as you have said, many producers have a hard time going twenty miles to see a new musical. What drew you to Toronto? And which incarnation did you see?*

### Roy Miller

*I saw the third incarnation, the third and final Canadian production at the Winter Garden Theatre, which the Mirvishes produced. And I was sent an invitation from the Mirvishes to come up and see it. I think the headline on one of the reviews was IS* CHAPERONE *BROADWAY BOUND? And I read the first paragraph, and it completely intrigued me.*

*It wasn't like anything I had ever seen or heard about before. It was simply the conceit of the show, in that a man puts his favorite record, his favorite cast recording on his record player, and it comes to life in his apartment, in his mind. And I thought,* How interesting. *I would love to see how that plays out, all the while thinking,* I can't imagine that this isn't too inside for a mainstream audience.

*So, I went up there because I thought,* Well, the reviews are terrific. But I'm also curious to see how a full audience reacts to it. *I flew up in July of 2002, and saw the final weekend, the final performances, and saw the audiences reacting, similarly to how they're reacting now—quite good. And I was just overwhelmed with the show.*

*I came back to New York, and I endeavored to secure the rights. But as much as I loved the show, I had always recognized that it really is about the Man in Chair. And I spoke with the agent and I said, "I would love to try to secure rights, but I really don't want to do the show unless I have some sort of good-faith agreement with Bob Martin that he would be willing to star on Broadway—if we were ever so lucky to get there."*

*I didn't want to find out after the fact that he wasn't interested, because I never would have gone after the rights otherwise.*

ATW

*Were there other producers seeking the rights? Were you in competition?*

Roy Miller

*I'm happy to say, I did not have any idea who else was going after the rights, and it probably would have made me a nervous wreck if I knew. Honestly, I never cared to ask the question after I obtained the rights.*

ATW

*What about the rights process?*

Roy Miller

*Part of the process was frustrating for me, since I was producing six shows a year at Paper Mill Playhouse. Plus, right after I secured the rights I was in the process of bringing* I'm Not

Rappaport *to Broadway, with Judd Hirsch and Ben Vereen. I had told the* Chaperone *team this would slow things down a little.*

*I knew that I wanted to do* Chaperone *in one or two regional theatres to see how a U.S. audience would react to it. I knew it was probably not the best choice for Paper Mill, simply because of its proximity to New York. I sent it to Michael Ritchie, who was up at the Williamstown Theatre Festival at the time, and a number of other folks. Also, just out of idle curiosity, I entered it into the National Alliance for Musical Theatre (NAMT) Festival for consideration.*

### ATW

*NAMT is an organization that supports companies that do musical theatre throughout the United States. They sponsor an annual festival of eight to twelve new musicals, presented in truncated form, entirely for people in the theatre.*

### Roy Miller

*Right. This was two years later. I wanted to be in there so that my colleagues could look at this and tell me if I were crazy or not. And I was successful in pretty much getting everyone from the industry, not just the regional theatres from around the country that are members of NAMT, but my commercial colleagues as well.*

*It was a phenomenon to see the reaction that came from that room, in those two performances, not only from the audience of theatre lovers, but producing peers. And they actually had to cut the presentation short, because it went over so long, which caused a little more . . . .*

### Bob Martin

*. . . laughter and applause . . . .*

### Roy Miller

*Which was a great reason to have to cut us off.*

*That's how it all came to be.*

*We hadn't really brought anyone to the table. We hadn't identified a director. There was talk among ourselves, and we took what had been learned from Canada. When we were chosen for the NAMT Festival, the immediate thought was,* We have to get a director to do this. *There wasn't enough time. We pretty much had to cast without the authors' input since they were in Toronto.*

*I wanted New York audiences to see what I experienced in Canada. So, I asked Bob Martin if he would be able and willing to direct this forty-five-minute presentation—which he did, basically to get it up to speed.*

* * *

### Kevin McCollum

*We were just moving into previews of* Avenue Q, *and I had heard about* The Drowsy Chaperone *from the Mirvishes earlier since I also ran a large not-for-profit theatre in St. Paul, Minnesota, called the Ordway Center for the Performing Arts. But I could not get to Toronto at that time. And I saw Roy—we had talked together as colleagues many times. Finally the day before, he saw me at a restaurant and he said, "You know, I'm doing this thing tomorrow." And I said, "Yes." He says, "You know, it's at 11:15, can you come?" And I said, "OK, sure."*

*I sat there. I just watched and I fell in love with who the Man in Chair is. I didn't find the play to be a parody at all. I found it to be a window into every human being, in terms of what defines them. And I think that's the power of this show. It's about definition of self and how art and life have to cohabitate, to inspire you to keep going.*

*But I really said,* Oh, my goodness, this is not about musical theatre. This is about the tools we need to survive. *And I got very excited about that idea and all the levels it was playing. And just to say, about this forty-five-minute presentation, it was very choppy, it was very episodic in terms of structure. I didn't find myself laughing as much as just doing calculations in my head of where my emotion was going.*

*And then, because everyone was laughing so much, they weren't able to finish the presentation. So, there was no ending. Anyway, I fell in love with it, and I rushed down to the stage and said, "You know, Roy, give me a call. I see what you're talking about now. I understand it."*

*That next night, I met the authors and we had a nice meeting of emotional minds. I said, "This is great, this is a great idea. Yes, it could go right to Broadway, I think. But we need to find the right director. Don't do any more work on it until we really find a director"—because I have a certain theory about musicals, where they must start on the earth, end in the heavens, be about community, and must be driven by love.*

# 3

## What about the Money?

*Charles Strouse*

I'm always curious about where the money goes—and I've been on the inside. Where does that budget go? Sets today cost what a mansion costs to build in the Hamptons.

*Thomas Schumacher*

It was once reported, in a fine upstanding New York newspaper, that it was irrelevant to Disney how much the show cost. And that, actually, is not what we said or ever intend.

What we spend on a show is keenly important to us.

What we do believe, though, is it should be irrelevant to the audience what we have spent on the show. Whether you do a tiny, little two-hander and it moves an audience, or a very large-scale show like *The Lion King,* which I also produced, that clearly represents a lot of money on the stage—

probably not as much as has been speculated—this shouldn't be what you enjoy. You shouldn't enjoy it more or less because of that. You should enjoy the work.

Because of this, we've always felt that by not talking about the money we could get people to focus on the work. *Do you like the work? Do you not like the work?* It's very important to us.

*Thomas Viertel*

In the end it's all just people. It's true that they may be people representing large amounts of money. But sooner or later, you're talking to some guy from Miramax or some guy from New Line, or some guy from Universal, who's trying to absorb whatever is going on on a human basis.

I haven't found much difference between dealing with the investor who writes a check for two-hundred-thousand dollars and the person who works for a movie company whose company has a million dollars in the show.

*Elizabeth McCann*

It's a tricky situation because once we produce a play, our costs don't end. Keeping it on until it finds an audience is an ongoing problem.

*Barry Grove*

It was only the long-running mega-musicals of these last few decades that changed the perception even of what success means. Along with, of course, the change in costs that pushed—for the commercial theatre—recouping out to a further point, and therefore made running longer a more dire need than it had been before.

*Lewis Allen*

I never recall, when I worked with Bob Whitehead, ever—almost never—thinking about the money side of it, because productions cost $75,000 and it was mostly friends and people who worked in the theatre: they put up $1,000 or $1,500 or $2,000 and making money just happened if you had a good show. And now, as the cost has escalated, more and more you have to get people to come in with lots of money. And therefore, they want their names up there as producers.

And how much experience? It varies with them. But most don't know a lot about it.

*Emanuel Azenberg*

The inclusion of everybody in artistic and financial decisions is very helpful in a production because you get real input and you have no secrets.

*Richard Frankel*

People are still surprised about the number of names over the title in shows. Some of them are very active and work continuously some work just in various stages of the enterprise. And there are some people for whom it is the price of a large investment. But these shows cost ten-and-a-half or eleven-million dollars. There really is no other way to do it. And the system works, I think, very well these days.

It is almost impossible to run an enterprise this size with the legendary lone producer. I would like to see anyone running a show that spends a half-million dollars a week and keep track of all the marketing, and do all of the management and administration.

Those old shows used to open and recoup in six or seven months. If they lost money, they lost a relatively modest amount of money. These things can sink you. If you try to do them yourself, they can be career ending. So, people are loath to do it.

There is always a core or a lead producer, plus a few others who do the actual work. Everyone else generally are people who are involved in a great many shows, so their opinions are very worthwhile. They usually have something to add to the process. The risk is spread. And everyone lives to fight another day if the show loses—as opposed to being out of business.

### *Charlotte Wilcox*

Every theatre will, right off the bat, charge you for their payroll package—which is the stagehands, the box office, the ushers, the porters, the ticket takers, the theatre manager, the doormen. Whatever that cost is for your show, you pay a hundred percent of it. Then, they also will get a rent factor, out of which they pay their real-estate taxes and all of their overhead. They'll also charge you specific figures for things such as insurance, garbage collection, the security people that take your money back and forth from the box office. And then, they'll want some kind of a percentage that goes from dollar one, or a certain dollar figure to be negotiated, as their profit.

*Jeffrey Seller*

Loading into a Broadway theatre is your second-biggest expense.

Loading in is the process of taking your set, your lighting, your sound, and your costumes from the places in which they originate to the theatre and setting it up. You employ IATSE (the International Alliance of Theatrical Stage Employees) stagehands in order to do so—and by the way, all of them earn a very fine salary.

*Susan Stroman*

There is extra pressure, when you know that if you make a mistake you could be making a $20,000 mistake. When you are creating, there is that extra pressure of finances that I don't think was there years ago. Even a simple pickax in *Crazy for You* is $500. So if I order twelve pickaxes, I'd better use them.

*Bernard Gersten*

The basic cost of a workshop is the talented people who are working. They get paid very, very modest wages for that period of time, and there are minimal props.

*Thomas Viertel*

The key to everything is that you can overcome all of the economic disadvantages by the passion of your audience. People will pay whatever is needed for the kind of experience that theatre at its best delivers.

*Michael David*

It's always been fun to me that the idea of the theatre thinking about raising the ticket price a dollar is on the front page of the *Times*. *The New York Times* raises their line rate, and if it's anywhere, it's buried. And they just love—I mean, they salivate—waiting for us, too, even thinking about what the price of the tickets is. I must say, they contribute to that cost.

*Robert Barandes*

Start at gross, maximum gross potential, measure that against what it's going to cost us a week, which for *Damn Yankees* (1994) we talked about $380,000.

And then, I have to go to an investor and say, "Investor, this is how long it's going to take you to get your investment back at a hundred percent of capacity, ninety percent of capacity, and eighty percent of capacity."

How do I sell that? That's what a ticket price comes from.

## IN DEPTH: *Mamma Mia!* ™ (2001)

*(Included in this discussion are publicist Adrian Bryan-Brown; producer Judy Craymer; director Phyllida Lloyd; producer and co-author of music and lyrics Björn Ulvaeus.)*

### ATW

*You have a show ready and now it is time to raise the money.*

### Judy Craymer

*Just finishing the workshop, everyone knew that we must push forward with this. I have a co-producer, Richard East, who works with me, who lives in Australia. He wasn't in London all the time. It was then that he, myself, and Björn, Benny [Andersson], and Phyllida, said,* Right, we now really have to get on with it.

*We had to find a theatre, which wasn't easy. There was no room at the inn in the West End. And actually, it wasn't that easy to sell the project to theatre owners. They thought that we were trying to do an ABBA tribute show or it was the story of ABBA's lives, which I told them many times it isn't—and definitely Benny and Björn never would have allowed that.*

*There was no theatre until Cameron Mackintosh offered us one since* Ragtime *had just pulled out of the West End. He offered us the Prince Edward Theatre.*

*We had been thinking of a much smaller theatre. We'd been thinking of a twelve- or eleven-hundred seater, and the Prince Edward is a sixteen-fifty seater. And I budgeted the show and capitalized it at less than one wants for a sixteen-hundred seater. So, it was a bit of a white-knuckle ride at that time. We said good-bye to our contingency and just got with it.*

ATW

*Under the circumstances, did you ever consider opening somewhere other than London?*

Judy Craymer

*Well, it's funny you should ask because yes, during the whole three years we worked together we thought,* Yes, maybe a Fringe theatre, then maybe out of town in Manchester or maybe in Bristol. *And actually, it was at the workshop that Phyllida and [production designer] Mark Thompson were saying, "Let's just go straight to the West End."*

ATW

*Did you set your sights at that point around the world, especially Broadway?*

Phyllida Lloyd

*No, I didn't. Judy may have, but none of us really. Our ambitions were quite modest at the beginning.*

ATW

*What did it cost to open at the Prince Edward?*

JUDY CRAYMER

*Just under £3,000,000, which was quite a high budget—medium-high. It wasn't the highest in the West End at the time, but it was quite high.*

ADRIAN BRYAN-BROWN

*Today, that's about $5,000,000, right?*

JUDY CRAYMER

*Yes. Everything is much more expensive here on Broadway, and always has been. Ticket prices are also higher. We opened the show with a moderate advance of £2,000,000. It wasn't until we opened and the word of mouth started that the box office really began to pick up, even though we were quite happy with the two-million at the time.*

* * *

ATW

*You now come to North America. Was your Toronto financing by the original backers who had invested in the West End?*

JUDY CRAYMER

*All our original investors from London followed us to Toronto and the U.S. tour.*

ATW

*From a production standpoint, would each venue be a separate entity? Or is there one blanket company that is producing?*

Judy Craymer

*It's our company—Björn, Benny, Richard East, and me.*

ATW

*You are producers. But are your investors investing if Toronto is a huge success but, say, if San Francisco hadn't been? Is it the same financing that put the show on in Toronto and the West End?*

Judy Craymer

*Yes. If* Mamma Mia! *had not worked somewhere, of course, they might have jumped ship along the way.*

* * *

ATW

*I want to get back to the money, money, money in the words of the song. Let's talk a little about it.*

Björn Ulvaeus

*One thing I know, there was never any problem raising money for* Mamma Mia! *Everyone wanted to be in it.*

JUDY CRAYMER

*Well, they didn't at the beginning.*

ATW

*Once success has been achieved, everybody wants to be a part of it, of course.*

JUDY CRAYMER

*It was just a kind of select group, really, which took a risk—took the risk, and then took the risk to go on into Toronto and Australia, and all the other shows. We gathered some other investors on the way. And people are very keen to invest, which is nice.*

ATW

*Are you able to use the proceeds from the successful productions to finance, or are you taking new financing each time?*

JUDY CRAYMER

*Every production is set up separately, and every production we are obliged to bring in our original investors—unless they actually drop out. They are all individual [productions], but the same investors.*

ATW

*You had successes around the United States. At some point, you thought it was OK to try Broadway.*

### Björn Ulvaeus

*Absolutely. I felt we were closing in. And we were to come to this city with a reputation. . . .*

### Judy Craymer

*To start the word of mouth—which was always our greatest marketing tool.*

### Adrian Bryan-Brown

*It was a very unusual approach, which paid off big time. The idea of using Toronto almost as a tryout for Broadway and North America was extraordinary. I don't think anyone has done that before. To have been out for a year before you come to Broadway and North America with a major musical was an extraordinary strategy. And it really worked.*

### Judy Craymer

*When I first came to marketing meetings here, everyone was saying, "Oh, you can never tour in the States. You're not a Broadway–branded show." We had success in London, and with ABBA, again everyone said, "But nobody knows ABBA in America. But we soon discovered in San Francisco that they did.*

### Adrian Bryan-Brown

*I became involved about six months after the London opening. And I've been on the scene—the productions that have happened since then—focusing on Broadway. And I'd say the real challenge has been to keep the word out about the show without overhyping it—letting other people say the good words about it.*

*We made a conscious effort to get the American critics over to see it in London, to get their feeling about it there, to get their input.*

*The campaign has been bold, but it hasn't been at all* hype-y. *There are just ads to say the show is coming, not ads that say* ***ABSOLUTELY BRILLIANT*** *before we opened here.*

* * *

ATW

*To return to the money, money, money: How much did the show cost?*

JUDY CRAYMER

*It cost $10,000,000, maybe a few cents under to be exact.*

ATW

*That's from conception?*

JUDY CRAYMER

*Yes. Capitalized at $10,000,000. And a contingency—the operating costs are between $360,000 and $400,000 a week.*

ATW

*Now, what could you possibly gross?*

### Judy Craymer

*Over $900,000 a week.*

### ATW

*So, your investors are going to do very nicely.*

### Judy Craymer

*Well, we hope—we always hope.*

*The traditional deal in the UK is a sixty–forty split: sixty to the investors, forty to the producers. We mirrored this deal here—very generous, I hope.*

### ATW

*Tradition here being fifty–fifty.*

### Judy Craymer

*Yes. We hope we will recoup within a reasonable period of time, about forty weeks. It could be fewer, it could be more. In London, we recouped in twenty-seven weeks. We recouped on schedule for Toronto and the U.S. tour as well.*

* * *

### ATW

*I'd like to get back to the nitty-gritty. Do you have a lot of investors? Whom do you call upon?*

## Judy Craymer

*No, it's not a huge group. It's probably up to about eight investors—main investors. But then, also, on Broadway we have some Broadway investors. In Australia, we have some Australian investors. But it's quite a tight-knit investment group.*

4

# Marketing

*Chris Boneau*

Marketing in the theatre is, unfortunately, a new thing.

*Linda Winer*

I think the theatre was slow to pick up on the marketing techniques that the rest of the country and the world, the West, had been perfecting—for better or, usually, worse. And in one way, I think it's healthy.

*Margery Singer*

To embellish what marketing is, it's all of the techniques that go into selling your particular event—and that includes advertising, promotion, public relations, direct mail, telecommunications, group sales. All of that encompasses marketing.

Promotion is really the development of a relationship with a third party, and through these companies and their resources, they can use their techniques to advertise whatever particular promotion it is.

*Kevin McCollum*

I don't care how much you spend on advertising. If the experience isn't special in the theatre, it isn't going to work.

*Marc Routh*

One of the challenges that we have as producers is to let people know about our shows: and especially off-Broadway, we have limited dollars.

A Broadway show will spend $75,000, $100,000 a week to advertise. Off-Broadway, we spend between $6,000 and $20,000 a week to advertise. And I think there aren't a lot of shows that can afford to spend $20,000 a week. So, by that very fact, we are limited in our ability to reach out to people.

*Todd Haimes*

There have certainly been times when I've felt that the actors felt that we should have spent more money on advertising so that there were bigger ads. And even if we didn't sell more tickets, they just wanted to see it and maybe it would help their Tony Award chances.

*Fran Weissler*

Marketing, advertising, and promotion I think are everything. You can just think about yourself. If you're running for president of your class, or if you're running for anything, you have to market yourself. You have to promote yourself. There has to be a buzz about that. And it's the same thing with what we're doing. Before we open, there has to be a buzz.

*Jeanine Tesori*

I think the great thing about the chat rooms is the interest and the dialogue. The really hard thing, which I am trying to understand, is when people publicly discuss what is not finished. And I think when we're all working on three or four hours of sleep and someone calls you with these really hellacious comments from the chats, you just think, *You know what? It's just not fair. Wait until we open, then chat away.*

*Michael David*

Just in general, about marketing in the theatre—what you're really talking about is sort of efficient information dissemination. It's not just about selling. Selling tickets is the back end, but basically it's how you get information out there. And I think what's expected in the theatre without thinking about it is that what you do is you throw a lot of money at something. And the fact is, if indeed the Broadway Theatre is this combination of art and commerce, necessarily you have to sell tickets in order to keep the art alive or to protect it.

The difference between Broadway art as product as opposed to toothpaste is the fact that there are only so many counters you can be on every week and that's all. You can only spend so much money per week on advertising, marketing of any kind.

### *Jeffrey Seller*

When you produce the right show, eighty-five to ninety percent of your marketing takes care of itself, just by the nature of the show. And I think that a Broadway producer who does great marketing could probably pump it up maybe another ten or fifteen percent. And one who does a poor job may diminish it by ten or fifteen percent.

But I think our ability to effect it is smaller than other people may think, because when you are dealing with the theatre, which demands a time investment and a money investment that's that large, people go by word of mouth to that first eighty percent.

And if you have a good show, people will tell their friends and they will listen to them, and they will go.

### *Ken Davenport*

I'm a big believer in what I call *fan the flame* marketing: when you see a little something, you go blow on it so that hopefully it will explode.

### *Linda Winer*

A lot of the shows that continue to run do so on the basis of the size of their advertising budget, so that if you've got enough money to make a show review-proof, then you can run a pretty long time on the unsuspecting.

*Rick Elice*

Advertising is space that you pay for in various media—print, outdoor, broadcast. It is also space that you can barter for. You can trade tickets for space or for airtime. And publicity is getting as much free space as you possibly can.

*Jeffrey Seller*

Advertising is a subjective number that every producer has to decide. But the truth of it is that nobody's going to open a Broadway musical today without having a million-dollar advertising budget in its capitalization.

*Michael Kuchwara*

Do people care about quote ads? I think it's producers who care about quote ads, and I don't know if the general public does. I mean, they see them, it looks nice on a marquee I suppose, but I don't really take them seriously because I figure they've all been sort of strung together. They pick a word here, a word there, and all of a sudden it looks terrific.

*Charles Strouse*

Broadway has international attention, frankly. For stars and for authors, it garners attention from around the world. I remember when *Applause* opened on Broadway, somebody sent me a newspaper from Hong Kong, an English–language newspaper, the following day, which said LAUREN BACALL TRIUMPHS ON BROADWAY. In Hong Kong.

*Rick Elice*

What *Damn Yankees* had, as a sort of flagship number—and was tremendously exploitable through advertising—is the song "Heart." It's a song that everybody in this country knows on some level. It is a song that, because it's in the show, we were able to use in the advertising for that show without having to pay a billion dollars.

So, we were able to have the most wonderful jingle in the world. In advertising, they're called *jingles.* Onstage, they're called *showstoppers.* But it's the thing that gets people singing along in their cars or at home, or while they're in front of the television.

And it's great because what it does is carry over. Long after the commercial is over, somebody still has that song caught in his or her head, and then it begins to act like a one-two punch. The next time they see the ad or the next time they see the poster, they think, *That's right, that's what I'm interested in seeing.*

*Elizabeth McCann*

It's very difficult to reduce a play to a television commercial, radio commercial, or even a scene.

*David Stone*

I just did my favorite thing in a long time yesterday. We did the entire 2006 media plan for *Wicked,* which is a luxury certainly that you can sit there a year out. There was one ad in *The New York Times* for the whole year, and that simply is because we like to take out a Halloween ad just wishing everyone BEST WITCHES.

It's all about other media. But I think that you know so much of it now is learning how new technology works. I'm not a computer person—I'm a little analog myself. But I am having to learn this because it's effective.

Now, you know, in some of the markets we're on tour with, more than fifty percent of the tickets are sold on the Internet. So, therefore, we have to start doing more there.

We also watch when an ad is put into the *Times,* certainly the announcement ad is effective. But after that, I'm not convinced a quote ad increases ticket sales of anything else does. We're starting to pull out of not just the *Times,* but print in general. We see that radio works certain times and TV works other times.

*Jim Weiner*

The Broadway theatre pays more than any other industry advertising in *The New York Times.*

*Ken Davenport*

We all know that word-of-mouth is what sells tickets.

*Emanuel Azenberg*

One has to be very objective about that judgment: about, *Is the word of mouth good?* Everybody says the word of mouth is good—but it's a delusion. Sometimes, the audience just doesn't want you. And it's the public that ultimately makes the judgment.

*Elizabeth McCann*

Years ago, the answer to every advertising problem was a TV commercial. *Get on television.* You'd turn on CBS and you'd see six shows in thirty-second spots in three minutes. Then, advertising on television became so expensive, everybody got off television, and started putting up big signs around Manhattan. Now, everybody does discount mailings. And there is the Internet.

*Daryl Roth*

I'm involved with something that's a little alternative called *De La Guarda,* and we have rush tickets every night for students, because the audience is a much younger audience, and they can't afford a normal Broadway–ticket price. We have discount mailers for all shows. We have promotions that go out. We have enter-to-win contests. On the Internet, we offer discount tickets.

*Kevin McCollum*

I don't believe in test marketing. Some people do. I ask friends, and I ask fellow producers. "What was your experience? What do you think?" And I talk to the venues themselves. I don't have a focus group. But the thing is every major city, every city has a tourism board. And those statistics are easily available.

*Amy Nederlander*

What you do with a show before you come to New York, in terms of it going on the road, generating word of mouth, the out-of-town reviews, how you can use those in your marketing campaign to make it so that when you arrive in town or when you're going to be opening up your show, [is essential]: getting people to know what you are, what is interesting about it, why someone ought to come.

*John Barlow*

That's what a publicist does: spreads the joy. And when it's as widespread as *The Producers,* and when it leaps off the stage and off Forty-fourth Street and out into the mainstream media, you feel, as a publicist, it's everything you ever wanted. It goes beyond publicity. It goes beyond the press agent. You think, *You know what? I can quit now. It's never going to happen this way again.*

*Rick Elice*

The best copy line, the best advertising slogan that's ever been invented: SOLD OUT, YOU CAN'T GET A TICKET.

## IN DEPTH: *Hairspray* (2002)

*(Included in this discussion are producer-general manager Richard Frankel and producer Margo Lion.)*

MARGO LION

*As I was coming out of the disappointment of* Triumph of Love, *I had the flu and I rented a lot of movies, one of which was* Hairspray. *Somewhere a few minutes into the movie, I said,* Yes! This is what I want to do. *It had all of the ingredients that one wants for a show. It's about a larger-than-life character that wanted something and had obstacles to overcome.*

*And it was set in Baltimore, which is where I grew up. The other thing about it is, I thought, it had a very contemporary style—an opportunity for a contemporary style—and it had personality. One of the things I look for when I'm trying to select material to work on, to commission, is personality. Too much of Broadway, too much of, I don't know, entertainment in general, is too generic—just sort of template work. And the voice of John Waters is nothing if it is not very personal to him.*

ATW

*You had to get the rights from John Waters? Or from the movie company?*

MARGO LION

*Actually, the rights were held by New Line. I began negotiating for the rights in the fall of '98, and in the spring of '99, the rights agreement was concluded. And the funny thing about this—maybe I'm telling tales out of school, and I don't think so—is I found out in the negotiating process that Scott Rudin, who had suggested the project to me, had actually had the rights before me, and I had not known that.*

## ATW

*Where did John Waters come in?*

## Margo Lion

*New Line was emphatic about the point that they wanted me to meet with John, which I did. Now, John and I are contemporaries. We both grew up in Baltimore. We both grew up in very respectable areas of Baltimore. We went to very buttoned-down schools; and yet, we had never known each other.*

*When I had my first meeting with him, I was really apprehensive. I thought,* What am I going to talk to this man about? *Because* Hairspray, *as many of you know, is actually his most mainstream event.*

*And, of course, it turned out he is a total gent. He is just a wonderful man and we had a lovely meeting. And I asked him, actually, if he wanted to adapt the material himself, hoping that he would say, "No," since he has never had any experience in the theatre. But I needed to do that. And he said, "No." But we agreed—I gave my promise—that I would honor his voice in this material and I wanted him very involved from the beginning, and that I wanted him to feel part of the team, because the project wouldn't have the authenticity without that involvement.*

* * *

## ATW

*Have you been able to find an audience for this show that doesn't usually go to the theatre?*

MARGO LION

*Well, yes. We actually have started a lottery in which we have $25 tickets available. How many are there, Richard?*

RICHARD FRANKEL

*I think there are forty-five.*

ATW

*How do you get the $25 ticket, as a lottery?*

RICHARD FRANKEL

*You go to the theatre at five o'clock and they take names. Then, there's a lottery drawing an hour later; so, you don't have to stand in line for hours and hours.*

MARGO LION

*You never know, really, what a show is going to be. You can't imagine that, in terms of appeal. You hope it's appealing to a lot of people, but you don't really know.*

*We hadn't thought of this as a family show. But it turns out that this is a real family show. The demographic is extremely broad. We have kids starting at about age four or five who come to this show. And we have a rather substantial contingent of teenage girls who give their birthday parties there—and that's a lot of fun.*

*And then, we have traditional theatergoers. We've managed to appeal to a demographic that is particularly difficult, which is the twenty- to twenty-five-year-olds—people who don't, I think, usually go to the musical theatre. And they just love it.*

*Our challenge that we're really dedicated to meeting is to bring in an African American audience. This is something that's very important to us because of the theme of the show. This is a commitment that we've made, and we're going to work hard. We'll continue to work hard to try and do that.*

* * *

## ATW

*What exactly are you doing to bring in or further target the African American audience?*

## Margo Lion

*Well, this is a challenge. I think one of the things that we're doing is we have a radio campaign. We've brought in a lot of people from the African American community who are commentators on radio. We're doing some advertising in African American papers. We've had a lot of group leaders, group-sales representatives who sell tickets to groups, come to the show. We had a reception for them. Some of our cast members go out and perform in African American churches, at black expos. We're going to approach the sororities, the 100 Black Men of America. These are the kinds of outlets we have.*

*It's not easy. But I think mainly because a black audience, an African American audience, doesn't know what the theme of the show is. And that's what we have to get out. We also need to do more advertising on the radio with the music, particularly with "Run and Tell That!" or "I Know Where I've Been," so that the African American audiences know that there's something there that resonates for them.*

ATW

*What about making more tickets available to young people in the schools?*

MARGO LION

*Well, we have made a commitment to these tickets that we auction off every day, which, as noted, we have the lottery for, and we have the standing room. The truth is, we have a responsibility to our investors. And we have a ten-and-a-half-million-dollar capitalization that we need to return. So, we've done our best in this department.*

ATW

*That's an investment in the future.*

MARGO LION

*It is, and that's why we have the forty-odd tickets that we have for very reasonable prices.*

# 5

# Going out of Town

*Mel Brooks*

Let me tell you about the producers. There's always one maniac producer, you know? And he says things like, "Oh, we're not going out of town. No."

*Amy Nederlander*

When you take a new show out of town, before you come into New York, a lot of how that town—the local promoter—is going to receive even the idea and then go out and promote it, take into consideration what the show is, what the property is, who's attached, who's creating, whether the producer has a terrific track record or you bring in members of the creative team who have proved that what they put together becomes quite popular—there's a lot.

*Judy Craymer*

You feel that there's less spotlight on you opening out of town. But technically and physically for the production, it's a bit of a nightmare really.

*Susan Stroman*

We were running long with *The Producers* in Chicago. And the thing is, we were cutting things that actually worked. There were laughs and then we would cut. Then, the next thing would land even bigger, so the laughs would go longer. We would get ourselves into a bind because we were cutting really wonderful laughs. But the show would have been too long to bring back to New York. So, it was very helpful, to pick and choose what laughs we wanted, while we were in Chicago.

*Terrence McNally*

I've always thought one of the reasons the mortality rate on Broadway is so high is that the road has died. I've had plays on the road where we made enormous changes, and the show has come to New York and been successful.

*John Barlow*

Musicals out of town can be so dangerous because of the gossip and the word back in New York.

*Marvin Hamlisch*

What I remember about *Funny Girl* was it was basically not a hit out of town. We were in a lot of trouble. And watching people—that's the thing that you learn. It's watching how you solve the problems—if they can be solved.

*John Kander*

One of the things that happens when you get a chance to go out of town, which is harder and harder, or get a chance to work in front of an audience a long time before the critics come in, you find that song in the second act never really works. So, for a long time you attack the song. You rewrite it, and it still never works. Until it dawns on somebody that the reason that song in the second act doesn't work is because something didn't happen in the first act to prepare us for it.

*Daryl Roth*

We did a tour of Bea Arthur *(Bea Arthur on Broadway)*. Another way to ensure that the road on its way to New York works is by having a major person that is well-recognized out there in the world. They're embraced then, and you gain that steamrolling into New York.

*Fran Weissler*

I wish it weren't such an easy formula, and it is much less risk, as a producer and so forth. But if you have a name show and a name actor, it's going to sell tickets more than if you're doing Sadie Gluck in God knows what. It's going to sell tickets on the road easier.

*Peter Schneider*

For *The Lion King,* we went to Minneapolis as an out-of-town tryout, which I think is very important when you develop new shows. And the comments we got over and over in Minneapolis were (a) "You're not advertising" and (b) "There's not much hype." And we kept saying, *But we don't care to spend the money on the advertising because it's nice that people come see it, we're not there to have full houses.* We're not there, actually, to make money. We're there to look at the work onstage, and it's nice to have an audience to respond.

*Donald Frantz*

With *Beauty and the Beast*, we started out using the word *adapt.* And then, once we hit Houston, all of a sudden we realized the word was *transform,* as far as creating a new show and creating something different.

# 6

# The Revival

*Frances Sternhagen*

There are now more revivals of things because they're sure-fire, or the producers and investors think they're going to be sure-fire, than new plays.

*Dasha Epstein*

Because today there are so many revivals, and because of the costs having escalated for a ticket, I think that as producers we feel safer with a show that already has had affirmation of success attached to it.

*Cy Feuer*

Well then, I would like to speak up for the revival. What is actually being revived are the words that are written. This is what a revival is.

*Charles Strouse*

I've fought on both sides of whether revivals are good or bad. If you are asking, *Is it a good thing?*, it is putting money in my pocket. It puts money in authors' and producers' pockets. It makes money for the theatres. But they are a bad thing because I think the theatre generally becomes more barren. It is something I think about a great deal.

*Harold Prince*

Everyone is thinking about the theatre as a sure-thing bet. Hollywood suffers from very much the same thing. This year, we're told, it's going to be all revivals. Somebody has decided that revivals are a sure thing. Somebody is dead wrong.

*Edward Albee*

We did *Who's Afraid of Virginia Woolf?* on Broadway, in 1962, for a total cost of forty-five thousand dollars. Now, the revival is going to cost close to two million. We had ticket prices at seven dollars and now they're going to be seventy-five.

*Elizabeth McCann*

Four actors were all nominated for Tony Awards for the revival of *Who's Afraid of Virginia Woolf?* Sam Rudy, the press agent, and I are standing in this lobby at the last performance. Time to go in for the third act. We turn to go and some lady asks, "Are you going back in?" And we said, "Well, yeah." And she said, "Well, nothing much happens, does it? It's just more talk, isn't it?" And I thought, *Oh, God, my*—And the company manager said, "Oh, no. It's fabulous, because you find out—" But she goes on with a whole spiel about what happens in the third act. And the lady says, "Oh yeah, I know all that, because I saw the good version." And I said, "Excuse me. What?—" She said, "You know, the one with Liz Taylor and Richard Burton. That was the good version."

And I thought, *That's what we're fighting. We're fighting a very strong image of that movie.*

### *Paula Vogel*

What's terrifying to me is that I watch everybody's revivals and they're still telling the truth.

### *Theodore S. Chapin*

I hate the word *revival.* This year (1996), for example, we have *Hello, Dolly!* as a revival. Now, that's the original production and billed as the original production, with a different director, but basically the original sets, the original star. Then you have *Company,* and you have *A Funny Thing Happened on the Way to the Forum,* and you have *The King and I.* They're all different. *Forum* happens to be designed by the same designer who did it originally. And it's sort of the same floor plan and it's sort of the same scheme. But it's a different design. *The King and I* is not. *Company* isn't. I wonder if this word is the wrong word to use.

### *Nathan Lane*

If I have one regret in life, it's that we cut "Pretty Little Picture" from the revival of *Forum*. I think one of the things you're up against is that there are memories of an original production, when people saw it for the very first time, and you sometimes have to fight against that. Because even if they saw the show or not, or it's something that they have mainly heard about, it takes on a legendary quality.

So, with people like Jerry Zaks and Rob Marshall, they try to look at this piece of material as if it were just handed to them and ask, "How do we do this with a fresh eye?"

### *Donna McKechnie*

If the story is there, if it's in a human scale in some way, the people will come. And the little kids will come and see it, and the parents and the grandparents, because the story works. And if the story works, I don't care if it's 1946. It's more interesting. It enhances their sense of their tradition and their world.

### *Charles Strouse*

Everyone would like Donna McKechnie in a new show or Nathan Lane in a new show. What a thrill for everybody, this kind of collaboration. It's electric. It's fire.

Revivals don't give that feeling. There isn't the excitement of a new score.

Today, there are splintered audiences. Perhaps to get the biggest share of splintered audiences you go for the people who know works such as *State Fair* or *The King and I,* and hope they'll bring their children. But it's not the same as new theatre. I don't know whether anybody thinks it is. It's only happening because nobody's investing in new theatre, or very few people are.

*Joseph Stein*

I don't see there's any big problem between a revival and a new show, aside from the problem of economics. The important thing is getting [things] done. The economic problem is enormous.

*Nathan Lane*

In these politically correct times, it was interesting doing a number like "The House of Marcus Lycus" [in *A Funny Thing Happened on the Way to the Forum*]: "I'm there to buy the flesh," and it's interesting how an audience reacts to it today. I have a feeling it's very different from how they reacted in 1962. There were a couple of lines we actually took out because you just sense the audience gets very uncomfortable.

*Rob Marshall*

A lot has to do with tickets, don't you think? If people are going to spend that kind of money, it has to be an event. It has to be a proven quantity of some kind. It's a three-hundred-dollar evening. So, should I take a chance on a play that I don't know about?

7

# Unions

## *Kevin McCollum*

None of us is anti-union. We have great respect for everybody who works in the theatre—again, there are easier places to work. But I think all of us are anti-inefficiency.

## *Elizabeth McCann*

The founder of Cirque du Soleil said to me one day, "I couldn't have created on Broadway, ever." He said, "The union rules would kill me." I asked, "What do you mean?" He said, "Well, because if I'm on a roll and I've really got an idea going, and everybody's in synch and somebody says, 'It's five minutes and you're at the end of the four-hour call, and we have to break for an hour,' that'll kill the effectiveness of that rehearsal call."

He was much more concerned about how union rules impact on his ability to efficiently get the creative process going.

*Conard Fowkes*

Performers who are so-called freelance persons do not have a structure to move into the way that other professionals do. If you're a doctor or a lawyer, businessman, there is a structure that you enter. You go to school and you learn. Even if you're a lousy lawyer, you'll probably get a job. And you can expect to receive pay raises as you go along and receive the loyalty of the company for whom you work. And the older you get, the more money you get, and you can look forward to in retirement.

Performers don't have that. There is no structure. It's chaos out there. And the association (Actors' Equity), certainly for performers—and it may be so for the other creative elements in the theatre—offers a structure. And, of course, the most obvious benefits are wages and better working conditions.

Young performers entering the business now, should they work under union contracts, are guaranteed a salary. If there is a living wage to be made, Equity will see that they get that living wage.

*Emanuel Azenberg*

Principals and chorus is a union differentiation. And I have a real objection to it. It makes first-class and second-class situations that are unnecessary. But there is an old history of having a chorus. And many years ago, the chorus kids were abused, so they formed a group. It was called Chorus Equity, which ultimately merged with Equity. They want to maintain a certain identity, so it's called *the pink contract.* I always say, *Can't we change the color at least?*—so there's a pink contract, then a white contract. It's the bureaucracy of an industry.

*Barry Moss*

The Casting Society of America is a collection of professional casting directors who are attempting to become a union—for protection, for benefits. The reason we formed this guild is that everybody thinks that his or her niece's boyfriend can cast a movie or a play or a TV show, that it's such an easy thing to do. And we wanted to let the public know, and also people in the industry know, that there are certain people who have been in it a long time, who are professional, who know what they're doing, and they can put the letters CSA beside their names.

And so, there are strict regulations in getting into the union. You have to have on-line credit for several years. You have to have two letters of recommendation by other members of the association, and you have to be voted in by the entire membership.

*Dianne Trulock*

As a stage manager, I actually act as a kind of middleman between the actors, the unions, and the producers. And if indeed, at some point, they want to set up a rehearsal, the producers will have to come to me. They say they want to work on the day off. I say, "I can't do that. The union won't allow us to work on the day off."

*Julianne Boyd*

It's called *society*, so one would not ordinarily know SSD&C (Society of Stage Directors and Choreographers) is a union. It became official in 1962, when, as I think many unions and guilds were formed—when Bob Fosse said he would not go into rehearsal for *Little Me* unless he had a union contract. That's how the union was formed.

The producers, then known as the League of New York Producers, now the American Producers, said *OK.* They wanted Bob Fosse.

And oftentimes, I think, when the unions and guilds get anything it's because one person, whom the other side wants, says, "No. If you want me to work for those conditions or those terms, you need to give me this."

And in this instance, it was a contract. And Bob Fosse was instrumental and Agnes de Mille was very, very instrumental in the founding of the union.

*Charlotte Wilcox*

When you set the show up, there are rules that are really not written down clearly, as to how many people you need to do how many jobs. It has to do with how many different things are happening at once, on the fly floor, say. If you have eight things moving at once, you need eight men. You can manipulate that to a certain extent. And when you get down to a crunch, you really have to negotiate each separate situation with the union head and bargain it out.

*Dean Brown*

United Scenic Artists cover sets, lights, and costumes. Each contract is different, depending on the number of characters, the number of costumes, the number of sets, whether the set is multiple.

There is a floor, but it varies. And one problem, or plus, on Broadway these days is it's basically the same ten designers doing everything.

*Berenice Weiler*

The one thing that the unions do have is the portable-pension and the portable-health plan, which means that you get paid wherever you go—each employer pays into the unions' plan. That has been really the greatest thing that's happened.

*Edward Albee*

The playwright is protected in the Dramatists Guild of America contract, but so is the producer. The playwright cannot enormously change his script once it has been optioned unless the producer agrees.

*Tisa Chang*

The size of the theatre and the number of seats are actually quite relevant to the scope of your project since the unions categorize what level you're going to be working on, which contract with the actors and with the other unions. Broadway, I think, is characterized as five-hundred and up. Off-Broadway is a hundred to four-ninety-nine. Off-off Broadway is under ninety-nine.

*Julianne Boyd*

To me, one of the problems on Forty-second Street is almost not Disney and Livent, but the other producers who won't negotiate with us. As a union member, I'm going to forget whether I like them or dislike them. And my job, as president of SSD&C, is to get contracts for our members. If they'll negotiate with us, and if they negotiate fairly and the negotiations proceed, whether we win or lose, if we all come with a compromise, fine.

But it's the ones who won't negotiate that we mind. There are some producers getting involved on Forty-second Street who are turning their backs on the unions. This, I think, may be—I don't want to say a more difficult problem, but it's certainly something we have to look at.

# 8

## Broadway and off-Broadway

*Barry Grove*

Broadway is not, by definition, perforce, commercial or non-commercial. It's a piece of geographic real estate.

*Nancy Nagel Gibbs*

Off-Broadway is actually a defined area by Equity.

*Marc Routh*

We call it *off-Broadway*. Whoever came up with that term was a horrible marketing person. It says *off* in the title.

*Fran Weissler*

There are three major theatre owners: the Jujamcyns, the Nederlanders, and the Shuberts. If you're producing for

Broadway, you have to work in any of those three establishments. When they're in trouble, and there aren't too many shows coming in—and there are other shows that look like they may close—they love you. They court you.

*Paula Vogel*

I saw this off-Broadway production and it was everything that you look for in a new play. It told us a truth that had my hands shaking. I was shaking. So, it's very interesting what plays are done off-Broadway, versus what's done commercially.

*Thomas Viertel*

When we started in this business years ago, we were off-Broadway producers, and we produced a string of shows off-Broadway. And that was a very good environment to produce in. We did several plays by Pete (A. R.) Gurney, and we did a play by Alfred Uhry and one by Terrence McNally. And you could make commercial sense out of those plays. It was a good way to build our careers, but it was also a circumstance in which you could actually have a successful run with a play.

That's completely disappeared.

It's funny, because in those days, everybody would say, "Oh, my goodness, if this play were ten years ago," this is back in the '80s, "it would have been on Broadway." Now, they are all on Broadway, and everybody's saying, "Ten years ago, this would have been off-Broadway." But the result is that the stakes are so high. You're talking about two-million dollars to produce a play on Broadway.

The stakes are now so high and the audience is so diminished that nothing but the single outstanding event actually succeeds.

### *Ken Davenport*

I sat down at a union negotiation where I said, "OK, we have to address certain issues." And the representative turned to me and said, "Come on. Everyone knows you can't make any money off-Broadway."

### *Lynne Meadow*

When you're seeing a show on Broadway, obviously a producer has chosen to do a commercial show with a single purpose: to make money from that show.

### *Marc Routh*

What off-Broadway is is always changing. I think we go through cycles—Broadway too, where, all of a sudden, things seem to be working economically.

I think we are on the verge of the pendulum swinging the other way, and off-Broadway starting to work again. I think some of the things that are happening in the Broadway theatre are going to affect that. The shows are running longer. It's much, much harder to get a theatre. The musicals have to be done in the straight playhouses. So, it's very likely that straight plays that would have been done on Broadway are going to start to be done off-Broadway once again. As I've always thought, that's one of the best places to watch a play as opposed to a musical, because of the intimacy.

*Barry Grove*

There is another thing that is important to say about being part of the larger Broadway family, and this is that, unlike all of our off-Broadway venues, by doing a piece of work in the Broadway theatres that we have, you attract automatically, almost by definition, a larger audience—because there still is an audience of casual theatergoers, or regular Broadway theatergoers, who are finding their way to this work perhaps for the first time.

*David Stone*

When we were looking at *The 25th Annual Putnam County Spelling Bee,* it was two-million dollars to do it well at a large off-Broadway theatre or three-and-a-half-million dollars to do it on Broadway and have the exposure of that. Well, it was a no-brainer. And I think that off-Broadway is left, I'm sorry to say, with not the product that it used to have.

*Jack Tantleff*

What's happened, Broadway is evolving down into off-Broadway. So, off-Broadway is very much a commercial enterprise.

*Ken Davenport*

Off-Broadway tends to get trickle-down audiences, and we get trickle-down economics.

*Jeffrey Seller*

Off-Broadway, an actor is going to make five-hundred dollars a week and he's not going to be able to have a wife and children, and support them. On Broadway, an actor's going to make a minimum of thirteen-hundred dollars a week and he's going to be able to make a modest living. Same thing for the stagehands. Same for the musicians. The truth of it is that on Broadway, the practitioners of the theatre can earn a living. Sometimes it's a good living. Sometimes it's a great living. But it's always a living.

*John Pielmeier*

When I saw *Closer*, a play that I thought was wonderful, it made me quite sad at the end because I thought, *If this exact play had been written by an American playwright, it would not be on Broadway at this moment. It would be off-Broadway.*

*Alan Schuster*

Making us into an adjunct of Broadway—we will never win that battle because Broadway's always going to win. They're always going to have more money and more accessibility to the media.

We need to define ourselves for what we do best, which is more cutting-edge, more sophisticated, more intelligent material.

*Marc Routh*

Off-Broadway is a better place to discover shows, because Broadway, you put it up there, and it's either a hit or you just cannot sustain the economics for very long before it has to close.

Off-Broadway, the reason a show can take six months or a year to find an audience is that if the running costs are sixty or eighty-thousand dollars a week—which, unfortunately, these shows are, sort of best case probably—then you can lose a certain amount of money every week as that show finds its audience.

On Broadway, if you lose a hundred grand a week, after ten weeks you've lost a million dollars. And so, you just cannot sustain that. Therefore, discovery is possible off-Broadway, and it's not on Broadway.

*Alan Schuster*

The purest sign of success off-Broadway is full theatres.

## IN DEPTH: *Avenue Q* (2003)

*(Included in this discussion are producer Robyn Goodman; composer and lyricist Robert Lopez; puppeteer Rick Lyon; composer and lyricist Jeff Marx; and producer Jeffrey Seller.)*

### ATW

*When did your paths cross?*

### Rick Lyon

*Well, it's funny, because Jeff Marx and I had a mutual friend. And Jeff had told her that there was a puppet piece, and she recommended me. And I came over and said, "Hi, I don't know you guys, you don't know me. What are you doing?" And I ended up doing a demo of one of their songs in class.*

*That was four years ago?*

### Robert Lopez and Jeff Marx

*Four years.*

### ATW

*When did book writer Jeff Whitty join the team?*

### Robyn Goodman

*That was later.*

### Robert Lopez

*That was after Robyn and Jeffrey got onboard.*

### ATW

*Did you then do some readings?*

### Jeff Marx

*We did one. We had six songs, and we thought it was going to be a TV show. So, we put it on its feet.*

*A friend of ours was, I believe, associate director of the York Theatre. And he asked, "On some Monday night, would you like to come and use the theatre?"*

### Robyn Goodman

*But I saw you at the BMI Workshop for the first time. You did two songs. My friend from HBO said she had just seen these guys performing at BMI weeks before, and that I should check them out. It was the funniest stuff she had ever seen. I went up there, because I think it was the first time I'd ever been to BMI. That's how I remember. You hadn't done York yet, because you only did it once—correct?*

### Robert Lopez

*Twice . . . .*

### Jeff Marx

*Yes, for four nights . . . .*

### Robyn Goodman

*That's when I met with you, and I said, "This would be a great musical. We should develop it into a musical."*

*And you said, "No, I want to do a TV show. But thanks so much."*

*Being the persistent person I am, I didn't give up.*

### Jeff Marx

*We had stood up at this reading—we invited everyone we knew—and we said, "If you know anyone at Comedy Central or Fox, or HBO, please tell them about us."*

### Robyn Goodman

*You asked me to invite all those people. I invited Jeffrey and Kevin McCollum, and three or four other producers and television people. And out of all those people, the only brilliant ones who emerged interested in the project were Jeffrey and Kevin.*

*We got together. We didn't know each other that well, but we liked each other. And we said, "Let's develop it. We get it. Let's make it into a real Broadway"—no, actually, not Broadway at all, just "make it into a musical."*

### Jeffrey Seller

*Oh, I think there are three kinds of laughter. There's the "That's funny." You say it. There's the "You smile." And then there's the laughter that just takes over your entire body.*

*So when I went to the York Theatre, which is in the basement of a church on Lexington Avenue—at Robyn's suggestion—I witnessed six songs. And I just had that kind of laughter take over my body, and knew right away that I wanted to participate in bringing this show to its next step.*

* * *

### Robyn Goodman

Avenue Q *was probably for off-Broadway is what we thought. Am I right?*

### Jeffrey Seller

*Absolutely. Well, at first, we didn't know if the puppets would play to a Broadway–size house. So, we developed the show—we absolutely thought this would be a terrific off-Broadway musical and that would play in the tradition of the original* Little Shop of Horrors: *play at the Orpheum, Minetta Lane, or a theatre like that. That's how we imagined it.*

*I think it's an interesting thing about the theatre, which is that when you make a show, you don't know who it's for yet, and you don't know where it's going to land. Lord knows, we never thought, before we did it at the Vineyard Theatre, that* Avenue Q *would be a Broadway show. And of course, going backward in time to my past, I never thought* Rent, *obviously, was going to be a Broadway show.*

### Robyn Goodman

*Well, it's interesting. We invited a bunch of not-for-profit producers that we wanted to help us develop a show. And several of them asked, "Well, who's it for? What is the audience for this?"*

### Jeffrey Seller

*There's a good answer to that. Anyone who ever said, "I don't know who it's for". . . .*

### Robyn Goodman

*It's not for you.*

*I'm sorry, I took your punch line. I'm sorry, it just came out.*

*Anyway, [casting director] Doug Aibel couldn't make the reading, but he saw them perform at a benefit.*

JEFFREY SELLER

*He just saw one number.*

ROBYN GOODMAN

*Yes, he saw one number and he flipped out. And he called me; he said, "I made a big mistake not coming to that reading." He said, "I'm interested." So, we said, "Well, if you can work with The New Group, if the Vineyard and The New Group can do it together, that's OK with us. But you guys have to talk."*

ATW

*Isn't that unusual, for two not-for-profits to get together in collaboration?*

ROBYN GOODMAN

*Yes.*

ATW

*Was that tricky?*

ROBYN GOODMAN

*Well, no, because it turned out that they were old friends, which was a lucky break for us. Both are wonderful guys and wonderful producers. And in fact, doing a musical for either theatre was a big endeavor and an expensive endeavor for them. So, actually, pooling their resources helped them both be able to do it.*

* * *

ATW

*What about the unions? Is there a puppeteer union?*

Rick Lyon

*No, we're all Equity.*

ATW

*You therefore can have as many characters as you want without the unions?*

Rick Lyon

*Sure. Your role in the show is Nicky, Trekkie, you know, as cast. Your role is various roles*

* * *

ATW

*Once you decided to go to Broadway, who figures out the budget?*

Robyn Goodman

*Well, we did. When we narrowed it down, we sat way back in the last row of the balcony—to see how the puppets would read.*

*Of course, what we found out is that they looked better than people.*

JEFFREY SELLER

*When your face is orange, you have a decided advantage.*

ROBYN GOODMAN

*Their heads are slightly bigger—they're big as human heads, actually. And they read wonderfully in these smaller houses; and that was the delightful surprise.*

ATW

*Does the set get bigger? Do you add costumes?*

ROBYN GOODMAN

*Well, we chose the Golden, which was only about a foot wider.*

JEFFREY SELLER

*For all practical purposes, the proscenium opening of the Golden was the same as the opening of the Vineyard.*

*The front of the brownstones—*row houses *is probably a better term for* Avenue Q*—was virtually the same as it was off-Broadway.*

### ATW

*Did you use any of the former set?*

### Jeffrey Seller

*No, you have to rebuild from scratch. You have to have a union shop build it. At the same time, we probably could have used parts of it. You need to rebuild it stronger and sturdier when you're going to do eight shows a week, and play many, many, many weeks.*

* * *

### ATW

*I hoped you would talk a little bit about the marketing. Jeffrey, this is one of the things you are wonderful at. I wonder how you started the idea of how to market the show and what you've done since* Avenue Q *opened.*

### Jeffrey Seller

*The major dramatic question for us going to Broadway was,* Puppets or no puppets? Advertise the puppets or don't advertise the puppets? *And literally, Robyn and I, on Monday, would say, "We should use the puppets." And then on Wednesday, I would say, "No, we shouldn't use the puppets." Literally, every day we would go back and forth: Were the puppets a liability or an asset?*

ATW

*How do you feel about it now?*

JEFFREY SELLER

*I feel that where we are now, in which we, in print advertising, use a Richard Avedon photograph with three puppeteers and some of the puppets—I think that captures better than any other tool that we've had the exuberance and special qualities of this show—which uses both unique puppets, but uses them with performers who are flesh and blood and have bodies and legs and arms, and are enormously attractive performers.*

*So, we felt that when Mr. Avedon did that, that was the first thing that really captured what we were looking for. That's what we try to lead off with now—an image that conveys the exuberance of the show; the fact that the show will make you feel good when you go to see it.*

*In a nutshell, I think that's where we are today.*

# 9

# Not-for-profit and Regional Theatres

*André Bishop*

The myth I want to dispel—there used to be this myth that's gone now, thank God—that money was somehow bad for you. That somehow, nonprofit theatres were fine as long as they were small and poverty-struck. It was the *Chorus Line* model that we all remember. We all wanted, and I remember this so vividly in the '70s, to have our own *Chorus Line.* Not because we wanted to be rich; but we wanted to have money to do better work, which is what happened at The Public Theater. They grew, they expanded, they nurtured, they developed—they did all that, partly, because of *A Chorus Line.* We wanted that freedom, too. And now, a little money helps. You can pay people better. You can live in better surroundings. You can renovate dressing rooms.

*Bernard Gersten*

The first time that a not-for-profit theatre did a play on Broadway was in 1971, when *Two Gentlemen of Verona* was taken from the Delacorte Theater in Central Park, a free, not-for-profit theatre, and went to the St. James Theatre, a Broadway theatre, and went there totally under the auspices of the not-for-profit theatre and for its own benefit. That may have been a turning point, but I didn't consider it to be, nor do I consider any subsequent events to be turning points. They have been an evolution of a kind of reality.

There seems to be something derogatory in the idea that all not-for-profits lose money. Of course, we don't lose money, we spend money. The bigger loser of money is the government. So we don't lose it, we spend it. And the idea that not-for-profit theatre "loses" money—it always goes in quotes—and the for-profit theatre just makes money, is unreal.

Actually, the for-profit theatre loses about eighty percent of its money in that it fails to return all but twenty percent of the capital that is invested on an annual basis, in for-profit activity. It seems to me, they're profligate. There's always surprises when they lose money.

We, on the other hand, are such careful planners that we know that we will spend more than we earn, and we raise that in advance. It seems to me, we deal with the problem, the market problems of theatre, much more reasonably and much more realistically.

## *Julia C. Levy*

New York has been extraordinary, and it is because our officials understand that the New York theatre, both the for-profit and the nonprofit, is significant to the economic life, the quality of life in this city. It is the arts that draw people here. It is the reason people visit here. Theatre, in particular, is why tourists come and it's why businesses want to be here.

*Lynne Meadow*

In the case of not-for-profit theatres, there often are many reasons that we're making a choice to do a show—to support an artist, to do work of an artist today whom we think will do something interesting tomorrow.

So, to the extent that our audience is educated in this, it will make the theatergoing experience better. To the extent that they're more comfortable in their seats means that they'll come back to see the body of work. We're planning entire seasons, thinking this through. We're not just doing one show at a time. Any one of us in our theatres is looking forward. It's important to us that the theatergoer tries to understand that distinction.

*Bernard Gersten*

Anybody can assemble a private place, money, and will, theoretically; but more often they occur in the not-for-profit sector, in the not-for-profit theatre, perhaps, than in the commercial arena. Not because one is pure and holy and good, and the other is bad and evil and money-driven. That's not the reason. Those are just coincidental aspects.

*Gregory Mosher*

I think probably the most alarming thing in the American theatre right now is that for twenty-five years, the not-for-profit-theatre movement has grown and flourished to the extent that they are a group of theatres producing a lot of plays, and a lot of administrators making a lot of money.

By a lot of money, I mean a middle-class living.

## *Todd Haimes*

I feel more pressure than ever, in terms of ticket sales, to have stars. My experience may be different in this regard. I sense that it is. But I can tell you, just from the Roundabout experience, that stars mean more now than they did ten years ago. In other words, an equivalent show with equivalent reviews ten years ago, without a star, would have sold more tickets than that equivalent show would now. I know because we've had enough years and experience with these types of shows to see how important they have become.

So, the trick for us has always been not only to try to get the stars, and get these people who have incredibly busy lives and lucrative careers to work for a thousand bucks a week, but also, perhaps more importantly, to try to get them to not compromise their artistic work, but also to enhance the artistic work. Nobody would argue with the fact that having a star who brings an incredible star performance—however you define that, to whatever the work—is not a bad thing at all.

## *Bernard Gersten*

My theory of names is that they tend to act like shrink wrap around what they are the name of. I learned this some time back, and I learned it first of all, in relationship to an individual.

*Adolf* was always a very bad name for me, when I was a kid, until I met Adolph Green—and then the name *Adolf* shrink-wrapped around Adolph Green and supplanted Adolf Hitler for me. And it became a perfectly lovely name.

The next experience was with a show called *Hair,* which was the first show we did at The Public Theater. These guys came in, with very long and curly hair, and said, "The name of this show is *Hair.*" I said, "*Hair?* That's a terrible name for a show. Nobody will ever come to see a show called *Hair!* It's too dumb a name."

Well, I didn't prevail. And gradually, that name shrink-wrapped around the show *Hair,* and hair as something that grows out of your head was as nothing compared to the show *Hair.*

*Barry Grove*

There's now a corporate model, there are partnerships, there are consortia, partnerships between nonprofits and for-profits that exist. Many of the people in the commercial theatre began their careers, now that there is a nonprofit that's been around for thirty or forty years, in our world, working in different kinds of ways.

*Julia C. Levy*

Since having *Cabaret*—which we did produce, which the vast majority of people who saw it did not know it was produced by a nonprofit theatre company—that I think has changed the expectations also of the artists.

## *Amy Nederlander*

Where are the brand-new works coming from? It is from the not-for-profits, where one has built-in subscription audiences looking for new works, knowing this is what they're getting.

When you go into the larger commercial theatres—two-thousand seats, three-thousand seats—the ticket price is high, audiences want something that has been proven in New York to be a success, so that the odds of their enjoying their evening are much higher, or something that they already know, like a revival.

Finding something that's original going into a multi-thousand-seat venue, prior to coming to New York, I think is unique.

## *Virginia Louloudes*

I feel guilty that we're talking about money so much because we're not-for-profit theatres. And I think what we need to state clearly is that our value of success and how we define success isn't just, *Did we break even at the box office?* We're forced that way because of the economics and the fact that we pay people, and we want to continue to make payroll and pay ourselves and continue. It's this balance, and I think it's very hard for the not-for-profit producers.

## *Neil Pepe*

We did this play, *The Cider House Rules,* a few years back, and that had twenty-three people. And for a show that size in our theatre is difficult. Now, that show sold a lot of tickets for us, and that was fantastic. We came close to breaking even on it. But it really depends on the work. It really depends on the piece. So, it's hard.

In the commercial world, I think they'll just forget it. But it's an odd thing on our level. We're on a contract called a Letter of Agreement contract with Equity, which I'm sort of embarrassed about because it doesn't pay the actors at all. But the reason that we're on it is we can afford it, number one. And also we hope we can get a play with fifteen characters—we're going to do *The Cherry Orchard* this spring and that has fifteen people in it. And so, hopefully, we can do that and afford it.

### *Eduardo Machado*

The pressure is always on. And I think we have double trouble, or double gain, which is we're nonprofit theatres, meaning we have to represent the people we're being nonprofit for—both in what we pick and in having a ticket price so an audience can really come in.

A lot of the people that I would like to see in my theatre can barely afford a ten-dollar ticket. So, I think it's a double-edged sword for us, to try to figure out what to do, since we have a public duty that we also have to provide because we are not-for-profit. It's tough all around, representing everybody you're supposed to represent, and getting your audience to be able to come to see your show.

### *Julia C. Levy*

As nonprofits, all of us, whether we have a membership or we have a subscription theatre, we're all charging below-market rates to our subscribers—to our members—for our shows, which the for-profit theatre does not do. For the *nonprofit* designation, we have to provide some kind of service to the community. I would say it might be enough just producing great theatre, which is what we do, but it's also providing it at a reasonable price, which is what we struggle to do every day—and that distinguishes us.

### *Lynne Meadow*

Does an audience member, who is coming for the first time, really know that he or she is in a nonprofit theatre versus a profit theatre? I think in our first year at the renovated Biltmore, there were a lot of people who didn't know, and they thought they were coming to see a traditional Broadway show.

### *Todd Haimes*

You have to cram as many seats as possible since the costs are so out of control. At Roundabout, just to speak of our own theatre, we took two-hundred seats out of the Selwyn Theatre to make it more physically comfortable even though economically it wasn't the best thing in the world, because we wanted it to be a different kind of experience, and because as a not-for-profit theatre, we viewed this as one of our roles: to make the theatergoing experience comfortable.

Having said that, it is a constant battle when you have the single-ticket buyers coming into your quote-unquote hit shows, to let them know that this is something different from a commercial theatre. But we're always trying to do that because that's how we expand our audience.

*Ellen Richard*

At Roundabout, we get to know our subscribers, and they understand who we are. We market to them for contributions. We send out newsletters. In our program, it's pretty clear that we have contributors. We have a kiosk in the lobby for donations and help. And I think once somebody has bought a ticket from us, we have them, they're contacted, and we do get a chance, then, to say who we are—that we are not-for-profit.

*Thomas Cott*

At Lincoln Center Theater, we developed membership as an alternative to subscriptions, so that we would have more flexibility, and the audience would also have flexibility. Members join for a modest fee. And they can choose to see or not see whatever we offer them during the year. And they don't see everything that we offer them since we do a lot of shows. So, they pick and choose. Some people love musicals, some people don't.

*Elizabeth McCann*

It's very difficult these days for not-for-profits to take the challenge of experimentation since they're captives of their subscription audience.

*Bernard Gersten*

We also hope to entertain in a more complex way perhaps, on a broader range than simply to entertain. And if we fail to fulfill our artistic obligations and goals and aspirations, then we fail as theatre and don't continue to exist. To a certain extent, we have fulfilled our goal and fulfilled our artistic mission, because that provides the engine that sustains us, which is the money that's contributed—audiences that sustain us, and artists that support our efforts.

### *Todd Haimes*

For me, there is a definite distinction that every decision we make, we make with the artistic product first and the financial considerations second: sometimes, a very, very strong second—don't get me wrong, I'm not being naive. And in the commercial theatre, by definition, it's the financial pressure first and the artistic decision second. And in a way, that's their responsibility to the investors. So, there is a distinction.

### *Tisa Chang*

The plus side of nonprofits is that we are able to create our own projects, incubate them, develop them.

### *Fran Weissler*

What we really need today and are getting today are writers and people that are writing new shows. A lot of it does begin in nonprofit theatre, where people can take a chance—and we're not talking about millions of dollars on Broadway to invest in a new show that can fail.

*Todd Haimes*

If not-for-profit theatres hadn't been there to give those artists the opportunity, because something in their work struck you, the reality is nobody else would have done it. It's not as if the commercial theatre would have done it. And those people would have gone different ways, some of them to Hollywood and some of them to God-knows-where, not in the business—and a generation of playwrights would never have existed.

*David Stone*

What nonprofits do—and they do it better than we do commercially—is nurture writers, nurture artists. They can say, "We're doing your next play regardless of really whether it's good or ready or not." We can't do that. We have to make sure the play is great and the largest audience wants to see it.

It's no accident that *Death of a Salesman* or *West Side Story* were developed in the commercial theatre, because they had to be good or else people were walking out—out of town. And I think that the nonprofits are great. Not only do we sometimes move things from a nonprofit to a commercial production, and they develop artists and audiences, too.

Yet, I think that the best work has to be in the biggest possible venue.

*Charles Strouse*

Something has changed. That is out-of-town, whatever that is—out of New York—the so-called regional theatre, the not-for-profit, and the many cities such as Houston and Chicago, and so on. There's a passion for the theatre that was never quite present before, and as a grouping of actors, stage technicians, directors, and so forth. There are new theatre communities, which I sense are as active and passionate as New York.

### *Paula Vogel*

For me, a great thing right now is that there are a lot more holes-in-the-wall with younger producers, and that there's actually a vitality out in the regional theatre, as well as in the downtown theatre, of plays that run for three weeks, with plays that are done on a five-thousand-dollar budget, with plays that are being written by twenty-one-year-olds.

### *David Stone*

Sometimes, cities' interest in theatre is out of proportion of their population. Boston is one of the best theatre markets in the country. San Francisco is. They're not as big as Dallas or Houston.

### *Kevin McCollum*

I have a show in Vegas and *Spamalot* is going to Vegas. And my feeling about Vegas is that theatre happens when people show up.

### *Thomas Viertel*

The nice thing about Las Vegas, in theory at least, is that it can absorb almost an unlimited number of shows, because the turnover of people is immense. In San Francisco, the vast majority of people who are going to the theatre are people who live in and around San Francisco. There's a minor tourist component, but it's not a big deal. And in Las Vegas, everybody's turning over every 2.9 days. So, if in the last bunch, some of them saw the show, then the next bunch is coming in right behind them.

I persist in thinking that Las Vegas is very much a cyclical thing though. We've been through probably two or three periods in my lifetime when Broadway shows were a big thing in Las Vegas, and then a couple of them fail, and the whole thing disappears for a while and then it comes back.

## *Richard Griffiths*

The whole theatre thing is in such trouble in England. When I was a student—it was over thirty years ago—virtually every town over seventy-thousand people had a rep theatre. The money was terrible, but it was a job there. And all the cities had two or three theatres. And of course, London was chockablock.

And now, thirty years down the pike, all of those sources are pretty well gone. There are about twelve, fifteen regional theatres now. And the Royal Shakespeare Company is in serious trouble. And the National Theatre is on a big roll at the moment, because [artistic director] Nick Hytner has done fantastic things. But it's significant by its rareness. It's not as if this were happening everywhere. Everywhere is in decline. And there's a lot of denial about this—but in fact, it's true.

*Sean Mathias*

The great thing in England is that if you can work at the National Theatre or the RSC (Royal Shakespeare Company), you can earn a living wage and you do have a certain budget for your production, so you can do a physical production.

There are three different auditoriums at the National Theatre. One, the small Cottesloe; the medium-sized one, the Lyttleton; the large one, the Olivier; and the budgets are reflected for each play, for each production, so that they tend to be smaller in the small theatre, medium in the medium theatre, and larger in the big theatre.

You can work in a range of styles and express your own particular needs and ambitions within the building if you get in there. But there are also the regional theatres, which are also subsidized heavily, and a lot of young directors can start off there and start doing plays by Shaw, doing classics out in the regions, where, again, they are subsidized.

## IN DEPTH: *Thoroughly Modern Millie* (2002)

*(Included in this discussion are general manager Nina Lannan; producer Hal Luftig; director Michael Mayer; book writer and lyricist Dick Scanlan; and composer Jeanine Tesori.)*

### Hal Luftig

*Annie Hamburger was taking over the La Jolla Playhouse. And she saw our reading and said, "This would be great. I would love to have this as part of my first season at the La Jolla Playhouse. This could be our premiere musical." And God love the La Jolla Playhouse, they start a lot of shows there*—Tommy *started there,* How to Succeed [in Business without Really Trying] *started there. And she said, "I would love for this to be part of our season."*

*Their musical slot was almost a year after we had done the reading. So it gave us more time to do some writing; gave the producers time to go find the money to do it since there are so-called enhanced productions as they call them now.*

* * *

ATW

*How much money was invested at this stage?*

Nina Lannan

*Well, I think—just to put it in perspective—outside of the La Jolla enhancement, there was about $400,000 spent in the development of the show over a period of four or five years, which includes the little readings. It includes the little rehearsal times, the workshop . . . .*

Hal Luftig

*. . . legal fees . . . .*

ATW

*All of that was recoverable out of the production cost when you moved to La Jolla?*

NINA LANNAN

*Yes, it's all part of the capitalization.*

ATW

*And had the show ended before La Jolla, you would have invested $400,000 . . . .*

HAL LUFTIG

*. . . for naught, yes.*

ATW

*I'd like to get to the money part as it relates to this regional theatre. Where did the money come from? This was such a big undertaking. How did you go about getting the money?*

HAL LUFTIG

*Well, the same way that anyone gets money. The La Jolla production, even though it was a financial undertaking, from a producing point of view it was a great showcase. We were able to bring money people out to La Jolla and say, "Look at this."*

*And they came back to me and said, "This is wonderful. What's the plan? What are you going to do?"*

MICHAEL MAYER

*These are all theatre investors? Is that how you know them? Or are they from different walks of life?*

## Hal Luftig

*You know what? They are from different walks of life.*

*Personally, I found it easier dealing with people who had invested in theatre before since they understand the mechanics: how it works, how you make your money back—you know, the recouping.*

## Nina Lannan

*You should talk about the IPN, also.*

## Hal Luftig

*Well, they came onboard after La Jolla. We have a big piece of investment from this new group called the Independent Presenters Network or IPN. They are about forty independent presenters out on the road.*

*With the road changing its face as it has, a lot of markets are now owned by Clear Channel Entertainment.*

## Dick Scanlan

*And Clear Channel would be producers on this show as well.*

## Hal Luftig

*They came on as associate. This was a sign of how much they loved the show.*

*But at the time, in La Jolla, when we were just at the ground level of seeing where this money would come from, these independent presenters came out to La Jolla and said, "You know, this show would be great on the road. Our audiences, our subscription audiences, would love this. It has everything we're looking for: singing, dancing, great story."*

*They went down their checklist. And so, they came aboard as one of our producing partners—in investment, really—only to make sure that when* Millie *goes out on the road, it goes to their cities first.*

*That was a unique form of capitalizing a show.*

## Nina Lannan

*I think that this is the first time that they've invested at this level. We're talking about forty theatres across the country, each putting in about $25,000, $50,000. Small amounts: for the chance to get it first on their season.*

* * *

## ATW

*How did you get the movie rights to mount this production?*

## Dick Scanlan

*Richard Morris had retained what is called* the dramatic stage rights *when he wrote the film, which is not the whole story. That gave him the right to tell the story onstage, to use the dialogue, the characters, the plot. What Universal still retained was the use of the title—to advertise anything called* Thoroughly Modern Millie, *and the use . . . .*

### Jeanine Tesori

*. . . of the songs . . . .*

### Dick Scanlan

*The songs and the right to merchandise anything called* Thoroughly Modern Millie. *Clearly, one can't produce a show if one can't use the title: you can't advertise it, you can't merchandise it, you can't use any of the songs. So, Universal entered into a deal with the producers.*

* * *

### Hal Luftig

*It wasn't until really we got on the stage in La Jolla and we saw that nothing, totally nothing, worked. And even then, I sort of said,* You know what? It's their subscription audience. It's their problem, guys. You know, they have to have the performances. You'll be amazed. This is regional theatre. They will make this work, just [wait]. It may not be perfect, but they will make it work. *And it became clear, I don't know, a couple of days before we were supposed to have the first preview . . . .*

### Michael Mayer

*. . . they weren't going to make it work.*

### ATW

*Were you running up a huge bill? Was this a union operation backstage?*

### Nina Lannan

*No, it's not really a union operation. The problem is, when you're in that environment, that regional-theatre environment, you have to let them sort out their own problems to a certain extent.*

### Hal Luftig

*As a producer you make a deal with the theatre. Let's say the show costs $3,000,000 at La Jolla Playhouse. The theatre says, "OK, here's what we have budgeted. We have a million-and-a-half. If you want to have a production of* Thoroughly Modern Millie, *you come up with a million-and-a-half dollars, and here's what you will get for it. You'll get to see the show on its feet." You'll get to use it as a sort of tryout, if you will, although things will change. You can use it to bring backers to see it, possibly to raise money.*

* * *

### ATW

*We were hearing a lot about the show here in New York when it was in La Jolla. The vultures were hovering. Had you hired press people at this point?*

### Hal Luftig

*La Jolla has its own press person.*

Michael Mayer

*We did have a press representative.*

ATW

*But you didn't hire anybody then to talk about New York—at least at that point?*

Hal Luftig

*We hadn't engaged anyone officially yet. But we did have a press person that we were going to use.*

ATW

*I think at the time, some of the job of your press person was to keep information out of the press in New York.*

Michael Mayer

*But the thing that was interesting was that the show was terrifically well received, from the very beginning. So, any press that was coming out of La Jolla, aside from just some technical glitches, was all extremely positive.*

Jeanine Tesori

*With the advent of the Internet, we all know what's happening. You know, with chat rooms. And I think there is confusion [about] what has been published—and typed gossip becomes believed.*

*It's almost as if people have become individual press people, and it's geometric. So, that comes out and I think that's a very difficult thing to rein in as a press person. That started happening, much to our favor, but any mishaps that were going on or delays became expanded.*

*They would come back to us, people from New York, saying, "Oh, I hear that you're delayed for three months." And we'd say,* What are you talking about?

* * *

### Michael Mayer

*Our first preview was a partially staged reading.*

### Hal Luftig

*La Jolla had the best intentions—they were more . . . freaked out by it because they are a subscription house. They rely on their donors and their subscribers, and their community. And when these people would show up, five, six-hundred—I think it was a six-hundred-seat theatre—they would show up . . . .*

### Michael Mayer

*. . . and be turned away . . . .*

### Hal Luftig

*. . . with their tickets in hand—*I'm ready to see Millie! *They would have to go home.*

MICHAEL MAYER

*We extended several times. It was ten weeks and we extended.*

HAL LUFTIG

*Some of these people would have tickets for Monday night, and we didn't have a show. So, they would somehow pick the next Wednesday. And some of these people came back two or three times, never to see* Thoroughly Modern Millie.

*So, La Jolla was really, really upset by this. And they were trying every which way to get it done.*

*We finally stepped up and said, "You know what? We have a vested interest in making this thing happen, now."*

*When you do a regional production, for the most part, you're a guest in someone's home. You can't walk in there and say, "OK, this is how we're going to arrange the china." You have to let them do it.*

ATW

*But you extended?*

HAL LUFTIG

*Oh, yes.*

MICHAEL MAYER

*Once we started up—*

### Hal Luftig

*Great response.*

### Michael Mayer

*I think that their subscription drive that went on during the run of* Millie *increased their following-year subscription hugely. It was a very successful run.*

### ATW

*Did you know you were coming to New York?*

### Hal Luftig

*Yes. At one point during the La Jolla run, the producers—we—all made the decision that this was worthy of doing, and we were going to come to New York.*

10

# The Critics

*David Henry Hwang*

The critics don't affect the production itself very much, that is, what goes onstage. I think they certainly do affect whether the production lives or dies, and whether it has a life.

*Clive Barnes*

I remember someone once telling me that the job of a critic was to sell tickets.

*Bernard Gersten*

If you press the critics, they'll tell you that we [the not-for-profits] mean a great deal to them. I really believe this. In print, they'll just give the facts.

*Michael Feingold*

People deal with their idea of you as a critic rather than with what you actually are. One of the things you learn in criticism, I think, is to look at the production for what it actually is. That's always the challenge. *What did I see? What did I hear? What is it about? What am I going to say about it? What did it do to me?*

*Clive Barnes*

I often have people come to me and say, "I always know when I'm going to like a show—because you hate it." And you know, I think this is a legitimate way of reading critics.

*Melissa Rose Bernardo*

Ultimately, I feel my service is to tell someone if it's worth spending his hundred bucks on.

*Ellen Richard*

I think it would be great that if the critics didn't like a show, they could talk about that one show rather than going back and reviewing the track record of the last few years, good or bad. It seems they continually want to review the entire institution in their critical review of a show. Sometimes good, too, but very often not good.

*Robyn Goodman*

Our critics are not like the critics in England, who are quite supportive of a body of work and have a longer view on writers. Our critics are: *Good. Bad. It worked. It didn't work.* They don't tend to look at it as a whole career, as a process for a writer. It's kind of a make-it-or-break-it world here.

*Peter Marks*

First and foremost, [the critic's role is] to be clear about what they think. Express it in an entertaining way. I think that's an underrated quality today, maybe different from what it was thirty years ago or forty years ago, when there was this notion of received opinion from a few outlets.

I think the value of a critic today is as much being able to reach people and make them feel something for this art form that, to many people, is a more remote thing than it was a generation ago.

*Susan Gallin*

The whole difference in what's happening now is that you can do a musical, and if there's an audience for it, you will have that audience. It doesn't matter what happens with the critics. With a play, there isn't enough of an audience. So, if *The New York Times*, and we've done this—it's not the critics' fault, it's our fault—if *The New York Times* doesn't like your play, you'll run for six months and that's it.

*Emanuel Azenberg*

In the long run, even *The New York Times* cannot keep a show that the public doesn't want running.

## *Clive Barnes*

I always found out very early on that in this business, you have to be able to cut the throat of your grandmother.

## *Linda Winer*

Clearly, there are no such things as objective opinions. When people say, "Gee, I want an objective review," well, it's nonsense. It's an oxymoron.

## *Michael Feingold*

Where do you separate? Is it the author? The director? The actor? It's only after experience, after repeated viewings of somebody's work that you get to understand that.

## *Peter Marks*

I was terrified at first at the idea of holding forth in the pages of *The New York Times.* And it took me a few times before I could actually look at my own reviews. Sometimes, I'd pick them up and ask, *Who is writing this stuff? Who* is *this guy? I mean, where does he come off?*

Slowly, you learn to accept that you're just one person who happens to be given this opportunity. And you try to be humble about it and not too grandiose. Over time, you realize that you hope the world out there understands that anybody, basically, could be expressing an opinion. It's just a matter of how well you express it.

*Robert Prosky*

I would like to have the critics have their say, but then just get a journeyman, an intelligent, well-informed theatergoer, or maybe a journalist right next to the critic's review.

*Elysa Gardner*

This is the nature of theatre that people who are going to be seeing the show are likely going to be seeing it once. It isn't a CD people will listen to repeatedly. Maybe that's just how I manage not to be too hard on myself. I think with theatre, as much as any art—or more than any art form—it really is about the impact at the moment. That's something I learn increasingly. It's important not to second guess yourself too much.

*Clive Barnes*

Who hasn't wanted to write a review over? Yes, but you don't have the opportunity to re-see the show.

*Michael Kuchwara*

My editors keep saying, "Shorter. Shorter." Newsprint is getting more expensive. They want smaller, shorter, reviews I would say.

Well, do you turn into a consumer guide saying, "OK, thumbs up. Thumbs down." Or, "You should spend $110.25 to see *Spamalot* or whatever?" Then, it just becomes about the money rather than the play.

I do have to say editors are fascinated with ticket prices. If I could put ticket prices in my reviews, that's one thing that's guaranteed.

*John Barlow*

Part of the reality of the bad buzz is the reviews. When you go out of town, you subject yourself to your local reviews in that market, and you subject yourself to a *Variety* review. So, you are coming back into New York with critics having weighed in. That's the reality. That's apart from the gossip or the editorial—you're going to be reviewed.

*Linda Winer*

I find that there's something called *emotional conflicts of interest,* which I think are much more dangerous than whether or not some producer takes you to lunch.

*Charles Isherwood*

Part of our job is being a reporter, conveying the experience of seeing the show, even if you don't necessarily love it. So that people—when they read your reviews, even though you are going to, of course, indicate your problem with it, sometimes if you describe it well enough—are going to know, *Whatever the critic thinks, I think I'm going to like this show.* Of course, also there's the factor that people who read you often are going to be able to gauge your tastes, your likes and dislikes.

*Michael Kuchwara*

If you misspell a name and your editor doesn't catch it, you'll have some snarky comment on some chat room saying, "Oh, they misspelled the name of so-and-so," this actor or the character played. And you'll hear about it, which is good in a way. I now triple, and sometimes quadruple check names of actors in *Playbill,* because you hear: the chat rooms, the people who read those chat rooms, are very passionate—sometimes way overboard. But they do keep you on your toes.

*Michael Feingold*

Before the chat rooms, there were the gossip columns. And if a musical starts out in San Francisco or Los Angeles with one production team and one cast, and it comes into New York with half of the production team gone and half of the cast replaced, you're bound to have to say something about that.

*Todd Haimes*

I always feel, and I may be wrong about this, this is purely subjective and anecdotal, but I don't particularly feel—my experience in other cities, both that I've worked in and that I've been in—that there's a certain embracing of the institutional theatres by the local press. I'm not saying that they give a show a good review if they don't like the show. I'm talking in the more general sense, supporting and recognizing the value of the institutional theaters.

I'm not sure I particularly feel that in New York. I don't feel hostility exactly. But I don't feel any sense of, *We have to make Manhattan Theatre Club and Roundabout and Lincoln Center and Playwrights Horizons and New York Theatre Workshop, we have to make those institutions succeed in the long run, even though we may not like individual plays, because they are very important to the infrastructure of our city, artistically and culturally.*

I don't really feel that, for the most part. I feel it's sort of cynical, an adversarial relationship.

## *Linda Winer*

If you take something that's fascinating for 500 people and make it boring for 500,000 people, then it's a crime against the art.

## *Michael Kuchwara*

The Associated Press, believe it or not, is a nonprofit organization. It's what they call a *wire service,* and we send our reviews out over the wire. They can do whatever they want with them. They can cut, they can run the whole thing. But it has enormous reach. Just in the States alone, I think we have about seventeen-hundred, eighteen-hundred newspapers.

I've seen my reviews cut to two paragraphs. So in that respect, I'd better say what I think of the show in the first two or three paragraphs, or people are not going to know what I thought.

## *Elysa Gardner*

You almost have to be more careful about what you write—that it won't potentially get taken out of context. If you write that there are *glorious costumes,* will they say GLORIOUS for the whole show?

*Roma Torre*

For television, we have to deal with two elements that my colleagues in the print profession don't. One is time, and the other is the picture. In terms of time, our reviews have to fit into a slot. Now, I'm luckier than most. My reviews must run three minutes or fewer. So, you have to get it all in, in that brief period of time, and there's so much to say and so much material to cover. It's very frustrating. The other issue I have to deal with is matching the pictures to the words. I was just telling Clive that it's often very difficult because I'm trying to broaden my horizons as a theatre critic and not do as much Broadway, and try to focus on off-Broadway.

The difficulty is that we have to shoot our own clips, and oftentimes the shooting is not very accomplished. And just at the moment, one of the characters is about to say something that is very momentous for my purposes in the review, the camera wanders off to another character or it pulls out of focus. So, it's very difficult. That explains sometimes why the reviews can seem a little disjointed or lacking.

*Charles Isherwood*

I have my own constraints. I don't have to match words and pictures, of course. I'm just dealing with words. But I am writing for an audience that is either working in or obsessed with showbiz. So, it's a very specialized crowd.

But, in fact, it doesn't really shape your critical response. That is going to be what it is. *Variety* does always address the issue of whether a show is going to be a box-office smash. If it's going to be boffo—which is a word we invented once upon a time, although certainly I didn't do it—or if it's going to be a flop. I think in consumer papers, you really would not feel right probably doing that. But that's something I'm allowed to do. Of course, that means that half the time I'm wrong.

## *Linda Winer*

I have on occasion been known to say, *Everyone around me seemed to be having a really good time. I wish I were there.*

## *Roma Torre*

I remember one of the first shows I had to review. I really wasn't sure what to make of it and I was getting anxious because this was one of my first reviews. And I remember a woman behind me who just chuckled, and she said, "What kind of cockamamie show is this?!" And that loosened up the whole creative process. And I realized it really was a cockamamie show and that's OK.

## *Linda Winer*

The danger, I think, in some cases, is that the person who's writing is much more interesting than the thing he or she is writing about. And pretty soon, that thing starts to sound maybe a little bit more interesting than it was.

*Clive Barnes*

Does it really matter whether you know the critic's opinion right away? It's only the press agent and the producers who want to know this. The world isn't waiting.

*Elizabeth Williams*

In fact, most of the big hits on Broadway didn't get good reviews.

If you have a good show, if you believe in your show, if you market your show, if you put quotes out from the reviews, even if they are not great reviews, apparently people remember the quotes and not the reviews if you're able to keep the momentum going.

*Peter Marks*

Usually critics, as many people may not know, are invited to review shows, and we go on nights designated as critics' previews. Once a show is running, sometimes we go back without alerting the production. I've done this on several occasions with the long-running musicals on Broadway. Just as the theatre is not a one-night deal, it goes on and on. We sort of serve it.

## *Daryl Roth*

You sometimes feel a little down if you put a play on and it isn't well received. And you're so depressed you think, *Oh God, what am I doing this for?* You say that for a while until you read the next play that excites you or until somebody comes to you with an idea.

# 11

# Final Illuminations

## *Neil Pepe*

Despite all this talk about money, I do believe that everybody here puts the art first. There are many shows that we go into knowing, *You know what? There's a good possibility some audience members might not like it.* But if I can stand there during previews, before the critics come, and say, "Not only do I believe in the story of the show, but I believe in how we produced it," then I'm happy.

## *Fran Weissler*

We happened to produce *Zorba,* with Anthony Quinn, and we took it on the road, we took it to Broadway where it played for four years. So, we really got to know each other. And for the first two years that we worked in that show, Tony would only talk to Barry.

And I used to come into Tony's dressing room and do the producer thing. I thought I had taste and was reasonably talented, and I would say, "Tony, you know, I think maybe you ought to do this, blah, blah, blah." And he'd say, "Maybe so. I'll talk to Barry about it." And he continued to do that for two years. He never addressed me. He literally never addressed me.

Now, of course, he was Mexican–Irish, and he had grown up in Mexico where women at that time walked three steps behind the guy. He really did feel that we belonged in the kitchen and the bedroom, and he didn't spend that much time intellectualizing with us.

Anyway, two years passed and I couldn't stand it anymore. So, I invited him to the Russian Tea Room, which was very big time then, and we sat in the first booth. And I said, "Barry and I want to take you out to lunch." So, he gets there and there is only me. I tell you that my heart was beating so fast. And this big guy comes in and everybody's asking for his autograph. He had this raw, animal attraction for everyone.

And he sat down and asked me, "So, where's Barry?" And I said, "He's not coming. You've just got me." And he asked, "Well, why isn't he coming? And he started literally to get up. And I remember taking my hand on his shoulder and sitting him down, saying, "Listen. I've spent two years with you. I really like you. I think you're wildly talented. But a lot of the decisions about what's happening in this show, I'm making along with Barry. I want to spend time with you. I want you to talk to me. I want you to recognize me. I know I'm a woman, but I'm not that bad because I'm a woman." I said, "So, let's start a dialogue."

We started to talk and we spent two hours together. And subsequently, he never stopped calling me.

*Alan Schuster*

I have to fall in love with a piece of material. If I'm going to spend two years of my life developing something, it's not an intellectual decision. It's a decision that I fall in love with the material. I'm willing to spend the time and emotion—and money—developing it.

*Bernard Gersten*

What we all attempt to do is balance what some people sometimes refer to as the four elements without which you cannot have a theatre: the place where it takes place, the money that provides the fuel on which the theatre runs, the artists who people the theatre, and the audience. Those are the four core elements of the theatre.

*Elizabeth McCann*

If you want to be in the theatre, the fun is never knowing what's going to happen, in a million dreams, in a million years.

*James C. Nicola*

So we stand, the idea that theatre is not amusement, but is actually a form to explore your essential humanity—which should be as essential an element of a community, as a library, as the town hall, as a school, as a hospital—is a relatively new idea. And I feel that the pressures on the artists—mostly, I feel this on the artists—to try and find a viable economic life infiltrates their creative lives unsuspectingly and starts shaping the projects to go down a certain pathway, without their even knowing it.

## *Daryl Roth*

You really have to work hard, and know that theatre is not the best way to make a living. Whether you come to it with less than worry about how you're going to make a living, it's still not the all-time best way to earn. People do it for different reasons. People don't do it to get rich. If you're lucky enough to have a successful play or musical happening, you can make a great success of it financially. But that really isn't the main event. That's the icing on the cake. That's the beauty of it. That's what proves the fact that all of this can really work in a financial way. But I don't think that's the impetus, nor is this the first priority for people to produce.

## *Kevin McCollum*

It's that great human experiment that you do when you produce. There is nothing as magical as the research and development of *What if?* And I think that is innately human. It's scary. It's exhilarating.

And to have that range of emotion in your business is rare, and it's why individuals are still there, because the corporation does not have those responses. A corporation looks at everything three months and decides, "OK, what does this mean?" It's a bottom line. And we are in a human bottom-line mentality when we produce.

And if we do that right the bottom line will come.

*Robyn Goodman*

Isn't it great that there's a whole profession where people do it for love? It's really extraordinary.

# *Cast of Participants*

*The following biographical sketches are, inevitably, far from complete. They are meant as a sampling of the work and credits of the people excerpted in this book. These notes focus almost exclusively on stage work—as well as, with respect to critics and union professionals, their connection to the stage—consistent with the theme of the* Working in the Theatre *series. Because some of those included appeared on the programs over the course of the past ten years, some of their credits in this section (circa 2007) may be more recent than their appearance on* Working in the Theatre.

Edward Albee is the author of many American classics, including *Who's Afraid of Virginia Woolf?*, *Seascape*, *Tiny Alice*, *A Delicate Balance*, and *Three Tall Women*. He has received three Pulitzer Prizes and the Tony Award for Lifetime Achievement.

Lewis Allen won Tonys as the producer of *Master Class*, *I'm Not Rappaport*, and *Annie*. Other productions include *A Lie of the Mind*, *A Few Good Men*, the Quintero–Robards *The Iceman Cometh*, *My One and Only*, and Peter Brook's *The Physicists.*

Emanuel Azenberg has produced more than seventy shows on Broadway including *The Lion in Winter, Ain't Misbehavin', Children of a Lesser God, The Real Thing,* and all of Neil Simon's work since 1972, yielding 134 Tony Award nominations and 41 Tonys. He has been a professor at Duke University since 1985.

Robert Barandes has produced several Broadway shows, including *The News, Epic Proportions* and *Bells Are Ringing*. As an attorney, he represented the original productions of *Grease* and *Torch Song Trilogy,* and the plays *Wit* and *Dinner with Friends*.

John Barlow is a partner in Barlow–Hartman, a theatre public-relations agency incorporated in 1999. The agency has represented over one-hundred Broadway and off-Broadway shows since then, including *The Producers, A Chorus Line, 700 Sundays, Movin' Out,* and *The Full Monty*.

Clive Barnes is drama and dance critic for the *New York Post*. He previously was chief drama critic for *The New York Times*.

Melissa Rose Bernardo is a senior associate editor at *Entertainment Weekly*. She has also been a contributor to *Encore, Where, Child,* and *In Theater,* of which she was one of the founding editors.

André Bishop was artistic director and literary manager of Playwrights Horizons before becoming artistic director of Lincoln Center Theater. His productions include three Pulitzer Prize winners: *The Heidi Chronicles, Driving Miss Daisy,* and *Sunday in the Park with George*.

Chris Boneau is a partner in the public-relations firm Boneau/Bryan–Brown, which has represented award-winning productions on and off-Broadway, regionally, and on tour. He is an adjunct professor at the Center for Theatre Studies at Columbia University, and on the board of the Atlantic Theater Company.

Julianne Boyd conceived and directed the musicals *Eubie* and *A . . . My Name Is Alice*. A past president of the Society of Stage Directors and Choreographers, she was artistic director of the Berkshire Theatre Company before starting her own theatre, Barrington Stage Company.

Mel Brooks wrote sketches for *Leonard Sillman's New Faces of 1952* and the books for the musicals *Shinbone Alley* and *All-American*. Then, for 35 years, he produced, wrote, directed, and starred in films, returning to theatre as the composer, lyricist, book writer, and producer of *The Producers*.

Dean Brown's costume-design credits include *Can-Can* (with Chita Rivera) and *Gigi* (with Louis Jourdan), and productions at opera houses including Pittsburgh, Cincinnati, Houston, Louisville, and Stanford. He served as a trustee on the Eastern Regional Board of United Scenic Artists, and on the National Executive Board.

Adrian Bryan-Brown has served as a press representative on over one-hundred productions on Broadway and off-Broadway during the past twenty-five years. He formed Boneau/Bryan–Brown with Chris Boneau in 1990. Their shows have won more than one-hundred Tony Awards.

Tisa Chang is the founder and producing artistic director of Pan Asian Repertory in New York. Originally an actress and dancer, she developed the company through work at off-Broadway's La MaMa e.t.c.

Theodore S. Chapin is president of the Rodgers & Hammerstein Organization; chairs the advisory board of City Center's Encores! and the Tony Awards Administration Committee; and is the author of *Everything Was Possible*.

Thomas Cott began his career at Alexander H. Cohen Productions before becoming a founding staff member of Lincoln Center Theater, where he was marketing director and director of special projects during his eighteen-season tenure. He was artistic director of Musical Theatre Works from 2002 to 2004.

Judy Craymer is the global producer of *Mamma Mia!* She previously worked for Cameron Mackintosh on the original production of *Cats,* and was executive producer of *Chess.*

Michael David is president of Dodger Theatricals and previously was executive director of New York's Chelsea Theatre Center. He has produced some 400 plays and musicals, including *Jersey Boys, Titanic, The Who's Tommy*, the 1992 revival of *Guys and Dolls, Big River,* and *Yentl.*

Ken Davenport is a producer of the musical *Altar Boyz,* and creator, producer, and director of *The Awesome 80s Prom.* He previously was director of creative development for NETworks and spent three years working with Livent.

Rick Elice was creative director at Serino Coyne, where he produced ad campaigns for some 300 Broadway shows. Since 2000, he has served as creative consultant for the Walt Disney Studio. An actor and playwright, he is coauthor of the book for *Jersey Boys*.

Dasha Epstein won Tony Awards as producer of *Ain't Misbehavin'* and *Children of a Lesser God.* Her other credits include *Romance Romance*, *Same Time Next Year*, *Orphans*, *Something's Afoot,* and *Mark Twain Tonight.*

Michael Feingold is chief theatre critic for the *Village Voice,* for which he has won the George Jean Nathan Award and been a finalist for the Pulitzer Prize in Criticism. He has also worked in the theatre as a playwright, dramaturg, director, lyricist, and translator.

Cy Feuer, with his partner of more than half-century, Ernest H. Martin, produced *Can-Can, Guys and Dolls,* and *How to Succeed in Business without Really Trying*. His directing credits include *Little Me* (with Bob Fosse), *Silk Stockings,* and *The Boy Friend.*

Conard Fowkes is the incumbent secretary–treasurer of Actors' Equity Association, a volunteer position to which he was elected fifteen years ago. He has been a working actor for forty-five years, and is also a founder of VITA, the Actors' Volunteer Income Tax Assistance program.

Richard Frankel has been the executive producer, producer, and general manager of a wide range of Broadway and off-Broadway shows including *The Producers*, *Stomp*, *Smokey Joe's Cafe*, *The Weir*, *Angels in America*, *Driving Miss Daisy*, and *Love Letters*

Donald Frantz is associate producer of *Beauty and the Beast* and *The Lion King,* and general managed *A Class Act.*

Susan Gallin is the producer of *Stomp, Woman Before a Glass, The Retreat from Moscow,* the revival of *Man of La Mancha, The Shape of Things,* and *Other People's Money.* She was the first recipient of the Robert Whitehead Award for Outstanding Producing.

Elysa Gardner covers theatre and pop music for *USA Today.* Prior to *USA Today,* she was a stringer for the *Los Angeles Times,* senior critic at *Rolling Stone,* and a Night Life columnist at *The New Yorker.*

Bernard Gersten has been executive director of Lincoln Center Theater since 1985, where notable productions have included *Anything Goes, Six Degrees of Separation, The Sisters Rosensweig,* and *Contact.* He previously was associate producer of the New York Shakespeare Festival.

Nancy Nagel Gibbs has produced *All Shook Up; Bat Boy: The Musical; The Big Bang;* and *Fully Committed.* Her general management credits include *The 25th Annual Putnam County Spell-*

*ing Bee; Wicked; The Vagina Monologues;* and *I Love You, You're Perfect, Now Change.*

Robyn Goodman was the co-founder and for thirteen years was artistic director of Second Stage Theatre. She is artistic consultant to Roundabout Theatre Company and has produced *Metamorphoses; A Class Act; Bat Boy: The Musical; tick, tick . . . Boom!; Avenue Q,* and *High Fidelity.*

Laura Green produced *Ten Percent Revue,* and is a general manager at Richard Frankel Productions, responsible for touring and international productions of *Smokey Joe's Cafe, The Sound of Music, The Weir, Swing!, The Producers, Hairspray, Young Frankenstein, Porgy and Bess,* and *Leap of Faith.*

Richard Griffiths won a Tony Award for his Broadway debut in *The History Boys.* His extensive stage credits in the UK include *Heroes, Luther, Art, The Man Who Came to Dinner, Galileo,* and *Volpone.*

Barry Grove is executive director of Manhattan Theatre Club, where with partner Lynne Meadow he has produced hundreds of American and world premieres. He is on the Executive Committee and Board of Governors of the League of American Theatres and Producers, and is a past president of the League of Off-Broadway Theatres and ART/New York.

Todd Haimes has been the artistic director of Roundabout Theatre Company since 1990, having served since 1983 as executive director. During his artistic tenure, Roundabout has received twenty-two Tony Awards and acquired three permanent homes, including the American Airlines Theatre and Studio 54 on Broadway.

Marvin Hamlisch won the Pulitzer Prize and the Tony Award for his score for *A Chorus Line*. His other Broadway scores include *They're Playing Our Song, Smile, The Goodbye Girl,* and *Sweet Smell of Success*.

Gregory Hines won a Tony for the role of Jelly Roll Morton in *Jelly's Last Jam,* for which he was also Tony–nominated as choreographer. His Broadway credits also include *Sophisticated Ladies, Comin' Uptown,* and *Eubie.*

David Henry Hwang won the Tony Award for *M. Butterfly*. His plays include *FOB, The Dance and the Railroad,* and *Family Devotions,* and he wrote the books for the musicals *Flower Drum Song, Aida,* and *Tarzan.*

Charles Isherwood is theatre critic for the *New York Times* and was chief theatre critic for *Variety.* Prior to that, he worked for *L.A. Style* and was senior editor and theatre critic in Los Angeles for *Variety.* He received the 2006 George Jean Nathan Award for Criticism.

John Kander, with his partner lyricist Fred Ebb, composed such musicals as *Flora The Red Menace, Cabaret, The Happy Time, Zorba, Chicago, The Act, Woman of the Year, The Rink, Kiss of the Spider Woman,* and *Steel Pier*.

Michael Kuchwara is the drama critic and drama writer for the Associated Press. Before being named to that position, he worked as a general-assignment editor and reporter for the AP in Chicago, and in New York on its General (now the National) Desk.

Lisa Lambert won the Tony Award for the music and lyrics of *The Drowsy Chaperone*. Her credits in Canada include *Honest Ed, The Bargain Musical, Ouch My Toe, All Hams on Deck,* and *An Awkward Evening with Martin & Johnson.*

Nathan Lane made his Broadway debut in *Present Laughter,* and has gone on to leading roles in *Guys and Dolls; Laughter on the 23rd Floor; Love! Valour! Compassion!; The Man Who Came to Dinner; The Producers; The Odd Couple;* and *Butley.*

Nina Lannan is the head of the general management firm Nina Lannan & Associates. The firm has handled numerous Broadway productions, including *Sunset Boulevard, Mamma Mia!, Thoroughly Modern Millie,* and *The Pillowman.*

Julia C. Levy is executive director at the Roundabout Theatre, where she was previously director of development.

Margo Lion's Broadway productions include *Hairspray; Elaine Stritch: At Liberty; Angels in America;* and *Jelly's Last Jam.* Her off-Broadway work includes *Mnemonic* and *Frankie and Johnny in the Clair de Lune.*

Phyllida Lloyd has directed theatre, opera, and television. Her international theatre credits include *Mamma Mia!, Six Degrees of Separation, Hysteria,* and *Wild East.*

Robert Lopez, with his writing partner Jeff Marx, created and wrote the music and lyrics for the Tony–winning musical *Avenue Q.* With his wife Kristen Anderson-Lopez, he wrote songs for *Finding Nemo* at Disney's Animal Kingdom in Florida.

Virginia Louloudes is executive director of ART/New York, the Alliance of Resident Theatres, the service organization for four-hundred nonprofit off-Broadway theatres. Previously, she was director of marketing at both Roundabout Theatre Company and Manhattan Theatre Club.

Hal Luftig has produced *Movin' Out;* the revival of *Annie Get Your Gun; Moon Over Buffalo; Jelly's Last Jam; Angels in America; Death and the Maiden;* and *The Diary of Anne Frank.* Off-Broadway, he co-produced *Lobby Hero; The Lady in Question;* and *Sex, Drugs, Rock & Roll.*

Rick Lyon designed all of the puppets and originated the roles of Trekkie Monster and Nicky in *Avenue Q*. He has worked on such diverse projects as *Sesame Street, Men in Black, Teenage Mutant Ninja Turtles,* and *Bear in the Big Blue House.*

Elizabeth McCann produced the Tony Award–winning productions of *The Goat, Copenhagen, A View from the Bridge, The Life and Adventures of Nicholas Nickleby, Amadeus, Morning's at Seven, Dracula,* and *The Elephant Man*.

Kevin McCollum has won Tony Awards as producer of *Avenue Q, Private Lives,* and *Rent*. He co-founded The Producing Office with Jeffrey Seller, and produced the regional productions of *Irving Berlin's White Christmas.*

Donna McKechnie won a Tony for creating the role of Cassie in *A Chorus Line*. Her Broadway credits also include *Promises Promises, Company, How to Succeed in Business without Really Trying,* and *State Fair*.

Ian McKellen has played classical roles both in the UK (with the RSC and Old Vic among others) and North America, with Broadway appearances in *The Promise, Dance of Death, Acting Shakespeare, Wild Honey,* and *Amadeus* (Tony Award). He was knighted in 1989.

Terrence McNally is the author of such plays as *The Ritz; Love! Valour! Compassion!* (Tony); *The Lisbon Traviata; Master Class* (Tony); *Lips Together, Teeth Apart;* and *Dedication*. He also won Tonys for the books of the musicals *Kiss of the Spider Woman* and *Ragtime.*

Eduardo Machado, artistic director of INTAR, is the author of nearly thirty plays, including *The Cook, Havana Is Waiting, The Floating Island Plays, Cuba,* and *Don Juan in New York City*.

Peter Marks is the theatre critic of the *Washington Post*. He worked as a reporter for *Newsday,* and was a reporter and feature editor for *The New York Times* before becoming theatre critic for that newspaper.

Rob Marshall received Tony Award nominations for his work as director and/or choreographer on *Cabaret, Little Me, Damn Yankees, She Loves Me,* and *Kiss of the Spider Woman.* He directed the film of the musical *Chicago.*

Bob Martin shared a Tony with Don McKellar as the book writers of *The Drowsy Chaperone*, for which Martin also received a Tony nomination as the Man in Chair. His credits in Canada include *An Awkward Evening with Martin & Johnson, The Good Life,* and *Skippy's Rangers.*

Jeff Marx won the Tony Award, with his partner Robert Lopez, for the music and lyrics of *Avenue Q,* which they also conceived.

Sean Mathias directed *The Elephant Man, Dance of Death, Marlene,* and *Indiscretions* on Broadway. His London credits include *Infidelities, Exceptions, Bent, Uncle Vanya, Design for Living, A Little Night Music, Antony and Cleopatra,* and *Suddenly Last Summer.*

Michael Mayer directed the Broadway productions of *Spring Awakening, After the Fall, An Almost Holy Picture, A View from the Bridge, Triumph of Love, Thoroughly Modern Millie,* and *Side Man*—the last two also in the West End—and the national tour of *Angels in America.*

Lynne Meadow is artistic director of the Manhattan Theatre Club, where she has produced more than 400 shows. Her directing credits include *The Tale of the Allergist's Wife, Woman in Mind, Ashes,* and *Moonlight and Magnolias.*

Thomas Meehan won Tonys for the books of the musicals *Hairspray, The Producers,* and *Annie.* His other Broadway shows include *I Remember Mama, Ain't Broadway Grand,* and *Annie Warbucks.*

Roy Miller produced *High Fidelity*, *I'm Not Rappaport*, and *The Drowsy Chaperone* on Broadway. He previously was affiliated with Paper Mill Playhouse, producing shows such as *Crazy for You*, *Follies*, *Gypsy*, *Chess*, *The Wizard of Oz*, and *Children of Eden*.

Gregory Mosher presently serves as director of the Columbia University Arts Initiative. A Tony–nominated director for David Mamet's plays *Glengarry Glen Ross* and *Speed-the-Plow*, he has been artistic director of Chicago's Goodman Theatre and Lincoln Center Theater in New York.

Barry Moss, both on his own and through his firm Hughes/Moss Casting, has cast countless productions, including *The Will Rogers Follies*, *Little Women*, *Titanic*, *Sophisticated Ladies*, *Nine*, *My One and Only*, and *Jelly's Last Jam*.

Amy Nederlander produced *Democracy*, *Salome*, and *The Diary of Anne Frank* on Broadway, as well as *Talking Heads*, *Tea at Five*, *The Santaland Diaries*, and *Tuesdays with Morrie* off-Broadway.

James C. Nicola is artistic director of New York Theatre Workshop, where he developed such works as *Rent*, *Slavs!*, *Homebody/Kabul*, and *Dirty Blonde*. He was an NEA National Endowment for the Arts Directing Fellow and later producing associate at Arena Stage.

Neil Pepe has been artistic director of the Atlantic Theater Company since 1992. His directing credits include *Sea of Tranquility*, Jez Butterworth's *The Night Heron* and Joe Penhall's *Blue/Orange* at Atlantic, and David Mamet's *American Buffalo* at the Donmar Warehouse and the Atlantic.

John Pielmeier is the author of the plays *Agnes of God*, *The Boys of Winter*, *Sleight of Hand*, *Willi*, and *Young Rube*.

Harold Prince produced such notable musicals as *The Pajama Game, Damn Yankees, Fiddler on the Roof,* and *A Funny Thing Happened on the Way to the Forum* before he began directing as well, with credits including *She Loves Me, Cabaret, Company, Follies, Candide, Sweeney Todd,* and *The Phantom of the Opera.*

Robert Prosky has been on Broadway in *Democracy, Glengarry Glen Ross, Moonchildren, A View from the Bridge,* and *A Walk in the Woods.* He has performed extensively with the Arena Stage in Washington, DC.

Ellen Richard was general manager and later managing director of Roundabout Theatre Company over a twenty-year tenure. She is currently executive director of Second Stage Theatre.

Lloyd Richards directed the original production of *A Raisin in the Sun*, founded the National Playwrights Conference at the Eugene O'Neill Theater Center, and was dean of the Yale School of Drama from 1980 to 1990.

Daryl Roth produced the Pulitzer Prize–winners *Wit, How I Learned to Drive,* and *Three Tall Women* off-Broadway. Her Broadway credits include *Anna in the Tropics, Proof, The Goat,* and *Caroline or Change*.

Marc Routh, president of the League of Off-Broadway Theatres and Producers, is producer of *Hairspray; The Producers; Cookin'; Stomp*, *Swing!;* and *The Weir*. A co-founder of Broadway Asia, he has produced *Stomp*, *Swing!* and *Smokey Joe's Cafe* in Asia.

Dick Scanlan wrote the book and lyrics for *Thoroughly Modern Millie.* A journalist as well as an actor, he created the role of Miss Great Plains in the off-Broadway musical *Pageant.*

Peter Schneider was President of Animation and Chairman of the Studio for the Walt Disney Company for over seventeen years.

His Broadway producing credits include the Tony Awarding–winning *The Lion King* and Elton John and Tim Rice's *Aida.*

Thomas Schumacher is president of Disney Theatrical Productions, having previously served as president of Disney Feature Animation. His Broadway–producing credits include *The Lion King* (six Tonys); Elton John and Tim Rice's *Aida* (four Tonys); *Tarzan;* and *Mary Poppins.*

Alan Schuster is a partner in the off-Broadway complex 37 Arts, and producer of *Marvin's Room, Oleanna,* and *Jeffrey.*

Jeffrey Seller is the winner of two Tonys as producer of *Avenue Q* and *Rent,* which also won a Pulitzer Prize. His other productions include *High Fidelity, De La Guarda,* and *La Boheme.*

Margery Singer has developed marketing and promotional campaigns for numerous Broadway and off-Broadway productions, including *42nd Street, Moon Over Buffalo, The Who's Tommy, Crazy for You,* and *Forever Plaid.* She previously was marketing director for Madison Square Garden Enterprises.

Joseph Stein won the Tony for his book for *Fiddler on the Roof.* He was also nominated for *Zorba,* and *Rags.* His other musicals include *The Baker's Wife, Juno, The King of Hearts,* and *So Long.*

Frances Sternhagen received Tonys for her appearances in *The Heiress* and *The Good Doctor.* Her credits include *Morning's at Seven, Equus,* and *On Golden Pond* on Broadway; and *Talking Heads, The Exact Center of the Universe,* and *A Perfect Ganesh* off-Broadway.

David Stone produced *Wicked, The 25th Annual Putnam County Spelling Bee, Man of La Mancha, Three Days of Rain, The Vagina Monologues, Fully Committed, Full Gallop, Lifegame, The Santaland Diaries,* and *Family Secrets.*

Susan Stroman has won Tony Awards for her choreography of *Crazy for You,* Harold Prince's revival of *Show Boat, Contact,* and *The Producers*, for which she also won as director. Her other credits include *Big, Steel Pier,* and *The Music Man.*

Charles Strouse has won the Tony Award as a composer for the musicals *Bye Bye Birdie, Applause,* and *Annie*. His other musicals include *All American, It's a Bird . . . It's a Plane . . . It's Superman, Golden Boy, Annie Warbucks,* and *Rags.*

Jack Tantleff became co-head of the theatre department at the William Morris Agency in 2003. Representing authors, composers, and lyricists, he founded The Tantleff Office in 1986, later joining Abrams Artists Agency in 2001 when that company acquired his firm.

Jeanine Tesori won a Tony Award for her score for *Thoroughly Modern Millie,* and was a nominee for her scores of *Caroline or Change* and *Twelfth Night.* Her musical *Violet* premiered at Playwrights Horizons and has been produced extensively around the country.

Roma Torre began her career as an actress and producer, beginning her TV career at Channel 2 News in New York, then working as reporter at News 12 on Long Island. Since 1992, she has been with NY1, as both anchor and theatre critic.

Dianne Trulock has stage managed such Broadway productions as *Master Class, Medea, Park Your Car in Harvard Yard, A Few Good Men, Othello, Lillian,* and *Sex and Longing*. She was associate director of the musical *Lennon*.

Björn Ulvaeus is a composer–lyricist and member of ABBA. Together with Benny Andersson, he has created *Chess* and *Mamma Mia!,* for which Ulvaeus was nominated for a Tony Award.

Thomas Viertel, along with his partners Richard Frankel, Marc Routh, and Steve Baruch, has produced the revivals of *Company* and *Sweeney Todd*, as well as *Hairspray*, *The Producers*, *Smokey Joe's Cafe*, *Angels in America*, and *Driving Miss Daisy*.

Paula Vogel won the Pulitzer Prize for *How I Learned to Drive*. Her many plays include *The Baltimore Waltz*, *Hot and Throbbing*, *The Mineola Twins*, and *The Long Christmas Ride Home*. She directs the MFA Playwriting Program at Brown University.

Berenice Weiler is a past secretary–treasurer of the Association of Theatre Press Agents and Managers (ATPAM). She was general manager of the American Shakespeare Theater for a number of years, and has general-managed such Broadway shows as *Wind in the Willows*, *Meet Me in St. Louis*, and the original *Nine*.

Jim Weiner is chief operating officer for Theater Mogul North America. He has been an entertainment-marketing executive for over thirty years, representing institutions from the Kennedy Center and the Washington Opera to numerous Broadway shows and touring companies.

Fran Weissler has produced numerous shows on and off-Broadway, including *Cat on a Hot Tin Roof*, *Zorba*, *Gypsy*, *Falsettos*, *This Is Our Youth*, *Annie Get Your Gun*, *Chicago*, *Sweet Charity*, *Full Gallop*, *Seussical*, and *Grease*.

Charlotte Wilcox heads the general-management firm The Charlotte Wilcox Company. Credits include *The Drowsy Chaperone*, *Dirty Rotten Scoundrels*, *By Jeeves*, *The Full Monty*, *Jesus Christ Superstar*, *Ragtime*, *Chicago*, *Grease*, and *Damn Yankees*.

Elizabeth Williams has produced the Tony Award–winning *Crazy for You*, *The Secret Garden*, *It Ain't Nothin' but the Blues*, *The Wild Party*, *Topdog/Underdog*, *Flower Drum Song*, and *Bombay Dreams*.

Linda Winer has been a theatre critic for the *Chicago Tribune*, the *Daily News*, *USA Today*, as well as dance and theatre critic for *Newsday*.

# *Index of Names and Titles*

*Italicized pages reference the quoted speaker.*

## *On the American Theatre Wing and CUNY TV*

Dedicated to promoting excellence and education in theatre, the American Theatre Wing has been intertwined with American theatrical life for the better part of the last three-quarters of a century.

Creating opportunities for students, general audiences, and even those working in the field to expand their knowledge of theatre, ATW is best known for creating the premier award for artists working on Broadway, the Antoinette Perry "Tony"® Awards. Given annually since 1947, the Tonys have evolved from a private dinner for those in the industry into a gala celebration of Broadway that is seen across America and around the world. Presented in partnership with the League of American Theatres and Producers since 1967, and broadcast annually on CBS since 1978, the Tony Awards are at once the highest recognition of achievement on Broadway and a national event that celebrates the vitality of live theatre.

Yet, the Tonys are but one of ATW's long-running programs. For nearly fifty years, ATW has made a practice of providing support to New York City not-for-profit theatre companies, as well as to students at select New York theatre schools, including secondary, college, and graduate levels, through its Grants and Scholarship Program. Each year, ATW makes grants in aggregate up to fifteen percent of the organization's budget, and over the lifetime of the program ATW has distributed almost $3 million in support.

In keeping with its mission of recognizing excellence, ATW sponsors the Henry Hewes Design Awards, acknowledging achievement in design from off- and off-off Broadway, as well as on Broadway, for designs originating in the United States. Conceived in 1965, these annual awards were originally called the Maharam Awards and later known as the American Theatre Wing Design Awards, but throughout their four decades they have cast a spotlight on all aspects of theatrical design.

The *Working in the Theatre* programs, which form the basis for this book (see the opening page), have captured more than four-hundred-and-fifty hours of oral history and insight on theatre, as the longest-running theatrical discussion series of its kind, offering sustained conversation between theatre artists.

Complementing these long-running programs, ATW has expanded into several new initiatives to broaden its reach. The year 2004 saw the debut of *Downstage Center*, a weekly theatrical interview show, produced in partnership with XM Satellite Radio. These in-depth interviews chronicle not only the current work of theatre artists, but their entire careers, in lively, free-ranging conversations.

In 2005, ATW introduced the Theatre Intern Group, a professional and social networking association of interns working in both commercial and not-for-profit theatre offices across New York City. Monthly meetings feature panels of experts exploring the opportunities available to young people entering the field, even as the meetings serve to build professional connections that will sustain the members as they advance in their careers.

The same year marked the debut of SpringboardNYC, a two-week boot camp of theatrical immersion, designed for college students and recent graduates aspiring to careers as performers. Over the course of the session, activities range from audition technique and finding an agent, to talks with prominent professionals, to advice on the financial aspects of working in the theatre and living in New York.

The American Theatre Wing maintains an archive of its media work on its Web site www.americantheatrewing.org where its media programs are available for free. This continually growing resource features more than four-hundred hours of audio and visual material that cannot be found anywhere else.

The current activities of the American Theatre Wing are part of a continuum of the Wing's service to the field dating back more than sixty-five years, when ATW was founded as part of the home-front effort to support, first, the British troops and later U.S. soldiers fighting in World War II. ATW captured the public imagination in the early years by creating the Stage Door Canteens, clubs for servicemen staffed by volunteers from the entertainment community, which grew and blossomed into branches across the U.S. and in Europe, in addition to a major motion picture and weekly radio program. When the war ended, ATW turned its attention to returning GIs by creating the American Theatre Wing Professional Theatre School, which for twenty years was a cornerstone in theatrical training. It boasted graduates such as Tony Bennett and James Earl Jones. At the same time, ATW brought theatre into hospitals and mental-healthcare facilities, as both entertainment and therapy.

From its wartime roots to its ongoing efforts to support theatre across the country, the American Theatre Wing continues to evolve in order to serve the needs of all who love theatre, whether they are students, ticket buyers, or those who create the work we all treasure.

CUNY TV, the noncommercial cable television station of The City University of New York, is the largest university television station in the United States. CUNY TV's arts, educational, and public-affairs programming reflects the community of the university to lifelong learning for all New Yorkers. Original programs are developed through partnerships with the city's leading cultural, civic, and business communities, as well as with international cultural institutes and consulates. CUNY TV reaches approximately 1.9 million households in the five boroughs of New York on cable channel 75, and each week about one-million people watch the station. Several CUNY TV series have reached national audiences through American Public Television satellite distribution to PBS stations. CUNY TV has received five New York Emmy nominations and one Emmy Award since 2002.